# Workers Compensation

## Guide

### Interpretation and Analysis

David D. Thamann, J.D., CPCU, ARM
Diana B. Reitz, CPCU, AAI
Susan L. Massmann, Paralegal

The
NATIONAL
UNDERWRITER
Company

The National Underwriter Co. • P.O. Box 14367 • Cincinnati, OH 45250-0367
1-800-543-0874 • www.nuco.com

Copyright © 2000 by
THE NATIONAL UNDERWRITER COMPANY
P.O. Box 14367
Cincinnati, OH 45250-0367

First Edition
 Second Printing, 2005
 Third Printing, 2006

International Standard Book Number: 0-87218-384-X
Library of Congress Catalog Card Number: 00-140011

Printed in the United States of America

# Acknowledgments

The authors wish to acknowledge the assistance of Anthony J. Kamnikar, CPCU, AAI, and William E. Rogers, CPCU, ARM, CSP, in providing information for and reviewing the chapter on financial plans. Tony and Bill are experts in workers compensation, and we appreciate their willingness to share their knowledge with our readers.

# Workers Compensation Guide

## Table of Contents

# Introduction

# The Workers Compensation System

## A Great Social Compromise

The workers compensation system was one of the triumphs of the industrial age. The system is the cumulative result of years of strife and compromise between employer/owners and employee/labor. The struggle toward this useful social compromise began in the 1870s with the organized labor movement and came to fruition in 1911 with the passage of the first state workers compensation law in Wisconsin.

In the workers compensation system, injured employees relinquish the right to sue their employers for employment-related injuries in return for a statutorily imposed mechanism that provides specific scheduled benefits. These benefits are funded, for the most part, through insurance policies that employers purchase from insurance companies. Indeed, in most states, employers must insure their workers compensation exposure or become qualified self-insurers. Employers cannot simply decide to operate without insurance. If they do, they risk being fined—and still have to pay the benefits that are set by law when an employee is injured on the job.

This work is a guide to the workers compensation system: how to calculate premium; how experience rating and modifiers work; and various financial plans and considerations. It also provides a detailed analysis of workers compensation and employers liability insurance by way of an examination of the standard workers compensation insurance policy. This policy is published by the National Council on Compensation Insurance (NCCI), and is available for use in thirty-seven of the fifty states. The remaining states use similar forms that are approved and published by their

1

respective workers compensation rating bureaus. The monopolistic state funds, federal workers compensation plans, coverage issues, and various other items of information are also covered.

There is perhaps no other type of insurance that uniformly affects the American population as much as workers compensation. Therefore, different types of readers may find different sections of this book of particular value. For example, human resource professionals, who often are charged with managing a program that a financial officer negotiated, may find the chapters on premium, experience rating, financial plans, and cost management especially useful. These chapters emphasize the correlation between program management and ultimate cost. Financial services professionals may gain insight into how to explain the system to current or prospective clients. Workers compensation adjusters should find interest in the chapters that deal with federal worker programs and general coverage issues.

The first chapters of this book (Chapters 1 to 6) examine the provisions of the NCCI workers compensation and employers liability policy, including its endorsements, on a clause-by-clause basis. How does the clause read; what does it mean? How have federal and state courts and administrative agencies interpreted it?

Many employers are located in a monopolistic state in which the employer is required to purchase insurance from the state fund. Chapter 7 details nonprivate workers compensation insurance—the monopolistic state funds of North Dakota, Ohio, Washington, West Virginia, and Wyoming. The workings of the residual markets maintained in some states are also mentioned.

Recognizing that state workers compensation systems were not adequate to protect all workers; for example, laborers working on waterways and on federal lands, the federal government enacted legislation such as the Longshore and Harbor Workers Compensation Act, the Jones Act, and other legislation protecting federal workers or workers on federal lands. Chapter 8 introduces and reviews federal workers compensation coverage—Longshore and Harbor Workers Compensation Act, Jones Act and other federal endorsements to the workers compensation policy.

Workers compensation is much more than an insurance policy. It is a *system* in the truest sense of the word; its cost is a basic cost of doing business. Because of this, the financial aspect of a company's workers compensation program often takes on a life of its own, outside the issues of coverage.

Chapter 9 starts the book's section on financial considerations involved in workers compensation coverage. Chapter 9 discusses premium and how it is planned for, calculated, and arrived at. Chapter 10 introduces experience rating and *the mod*. Chapter 11 reviews various financial plans; Chapter 12 analyzes cost management issues; and Chapter 13 discusses a number of workers compensation coverage and legal issues: exclusive remedy; dual capacity; intentional tort; third-party-over; etc.

This guide joins a number of guides published by the National Underwriter Company that review and analyze individual insurance forms. Among these are *Commercial General Liability* (sixth edition), *Commercial Property, Businessowners, Business Auto, Homeowners, Personal Umbrella, Personal Auto, Employment Practices Liability, Commercial Property, Employment Practices Liability,* and *Directors & Officers*.

# Chapter 1

# Policy Organization, General Section

## Policy Organization

The workers compensation and employers liability insurance policy contains three separate and distinct parts of coverage. What coverages are applicable are indicated in the policy's information page, which is the workers compensation policy's equivalent of the declarations page in other property and casualty insurance formats.

Part one is the workers compensation section, under which the insurer agrees to pay the benefits imposed upon the insured by the workers compensation law of the state or states listed on the information page.

Part two is the employers liability section, which protects the insured against liability imposed by law for injury to employees in the course of employment that is not compensable under the workers compensation section. Chapter 3 contains a discussion of why employers liability coverage is necessary as part of a workers compensation coverage program.

Part three provides other states insurance for workers compensation and employers liability coverage in states that are not listed on the information page for purposes of part one coverage and if the insurer is not permitted to pay benefits required by the applicable workers compensation law directly to persons entitled to them. This coverage applies only to those states listed.

## General Section

The workers compensation policy opens with a general section, something akin to an informative introduction to the policy. The general section contains five clauses.

The first clause identifies the policy as a contract of insurance between the employer (named on the information page) and the insurer. The benefits paid under a workers compensation claim may go to an employee, but the insured is the employer. In this way, the policy is a liability policy covering legal obligations imposed (in this case, statutorily) upon the insured. And, since the policy is a contract, this clause notes that the only agreements related to the coverage provided by the policy are those that are stated *in* the policy— no outside contracts or side agreements are to have an effect on the coverage. Of course, the terms of the policy can be changed or waived as any other contract can, but such modifications have to be accomplished by endorsements to the policy, endorsements which are issued by the insurer.

The first clause also specifies that the information page is part of (incorporated into as if it were an actual part of) the overall policy. The following data is listed on the information page: the effective dates of the policy; applicable endorsements; the insured and the insurer; the estimated premium; and the various states in which the coverage parts of the workers compensation policy apply.

The second clause confirms that an employer named in the information page is the named insured under the policy. The insured can be an individual, a partnership, a corporation, or some other entity. If the employer is a partnership, this clause specifies that an individual partner is an insured, but only in the capacity as an employer of the partnership's employees. The phrase recognizes the legal status of a partner; that is, it makes an individual partner an insured so that the partner's private holdings won't become subject to a claim by an injured worker.

The third clause notes that the coverage and benefits paid to the injured workers are based on the workers compensation law of each state or territory named in Item 3.A. of the information page. Item 3.A. is where the insured should list all states in which it conducts operations. The insured might have operations in more than one state, such as plants, retail stores, or traveling representatives; in some cases, major corporations have operations in every state. The insured might have one business domicile (the major place of business operations, or the official place of incorporation), but do business in multiple states; a business as noncomplex as a small plumbing contractor near a state border may have an exposure in two or three states. Or, the insured might not have multi-state operations nor employees that daily cross state lines, but may regularly send employees to lengthy seminars or meetings that are traditionally held out-of-state. In all these instances, the insured faces multi-state workers compensation exposures, and since the insured is charged with the responsibility of listing the appropriate state(s) or territory so that the proper benefits can be paid to injured employees, understanding and complying with this clause is crucial for insured employers.

This third clause also emphasizes the point that workers compensation coverage is applicable under and in accordance with state law, not federal compensation law. Quoting the policy, "The workers compensation law does not include any federal workers or workmen's compensation law, any federal occupational disease law, or the provisions of any law that provide nonoccupational disability benefits". Also, the "nonoccupational disability benefits" phrase shows that coverage under the policy is meant for injuries arising out of and in the course of employment, not disabilities that have nothing to do with employment; an example of this would be an employee of the named insured falling and breaking his leg while at home.

An additional note on this third clause: it shows that treatment of occupational diseases is covered under the workers compensation policy. The workers compensation part of the policy takes over the liability of the employer under the compensation laws of any state indicated on the information page, so any mandated obligation for occupational diseases is covered. Since the insuring clause of the workers compensation part of the policy refers simply to the "workers compensation law", and this term is defined in the third clause as including any occupational disease law, special endorsements are not necessary in states having separate occupational legislation. Listing the state on the information page takes care of all such liability under the compensation law of that state.

The fourth clause in the general section defines "state" as any state of the United States of America, and the District of Columbia. This does not mean that the workers compensation policy is applicable only in the fifty states and the District of Columbia. Any state *or territory* named in Item 3.A. of the information page shows the territorial applicability of the policy, but "state" is defined here just to clarify other paragraphs and phrases found throughout the policy. For example, if an employee is traveling in a foreign country on business, benefits for injuries suffered will be based on the workers compensation law of the state or states listed in Item 3.A.

The last clause in the general section declares that the policy "covers all of your workplaces listed in Items 1 or 4 of the information page; and it covers all other workplaces in Item 3.A. states unless you have other insurance or are self-insured for such workplaces." This clause shows the omnibus nature of the workers compensation coverage. If the insured has one workplace or twenty workplaces, this policy can apply; there is coverage if the insured lists all the workplaces on the information page. Furthermore, there is coverage even if the workplaces are not specifically listed, as long as the state(s) where the workplaces are located is noted in Item 3.A. Of course, this coverage does not apply if the insured has other insurance or is self-insured for such workplaces; otherwise, the insured would have duplicate coverage and that is something that insurers attempt to prevent.

# Chapter 2

# Workers Compensation Insurance

## To "Pay Promptly When Due the Benefits Required by Law"

This is the heart of the workers compensation system—the pledge to provide a statutorily mandated schedule of benefits to persons injured in the course of employment. Under this section of the policy, the insurer agrees to pay the benefits imposed by law on the insured employer arising from injuries sustained by an employee during and in the course of employment.

The workers compensation insurance section is part one of the policy. It contains eight clauses.

## How This Insurance Applies

Workers compensation insurance applies to bodily injury by accident or by disease. Bodily injury includes resulting death. The clause attaches stipulations to this declaration. First, bodily injury by accident must occur during the policy period. Secondly, bodily injury by disease must be caused or aggravated by conditions of employment, with the employee's last exposure to the conditions causing or aggravating the bodily injury occurring during the policy period. For example, in order for workers compensation insurance to apply to a worker who is suffering from lung disease, the insured would need to show the following: the worker's disease was caused by or aggravated by the working conditions (such as, having to constantly inhale smoke or other indoor air pollutants); and, the insurance policy was in force at the time the employee was last exposed to the conditions.

There are several items to note concerning this clause. First, the insurance applies to "bodily injury." The workers compensation policy does not define that term, however, and that can lead to disputes over the question of coverage should an employee make a claim based on mental stress. Is mental stress a bodily injury under the workers compensation policy? This issue is discussed more fully in Chapter 13, but suffice it to say that since the policy does not define "bodily injury," the individual state laws and court decisions will settle any dispute.

Another point to note is that the coverage is for bodily injury caused by accident or by disease. Just as a slip and fall injury at work is covered, so also is a disease-based injury, such as asbestosis or electromagnetic field health hazards—as long as such disease is caused or aggravated by the employment.

Finally, the clause certifies that coverage is provided if the bodily injury occurs during the policy period. This makes the workers compensation policy an occurrence-type policy, similar to the commercial general liability occurrence form.

## We Will Pay

In this clause the policy specifies that the insurer will "pay promptly when due the benefits required...by the workers compensation law"—a very simple and straightforward insuring agreement. Whatever the particular state workers compensation law declares the benefit to be, say for a broken arm, that is what the insurer will pay. A complication can arise, though, over the fact that an employee who is injured while working in a certain state can claim the compensation benefits of that state regardless of the fact that the employer is based in another state. In other words, an injured employee can choose among several possible states (depending on the laws of the states and the circumstances of the injuries) for his or her benefits. Just because company A is located in Maryland does not mean that an injured employee always has to file for workers compensation benefits in Maryland; if that employee is injured while on business in Pennsylvania, he or she could seek the compensation benefits of Pennsylvania.

This can seem unacceptable "forum shopping"—picking and choosing where to file a claim to get higher benefits—but in reality, such a practice is limited by the various state laws and by some judicial decisions, such as

*Bradshaw v. Old Republic Insurance Company*, 922 S.W.2d 503 (Tenn. 1996). In this case, Bradshaw worked for a Tennessee company but was injured while on business in Maryland. He filed for benefits in Maryland but was turned down; he then filed in Tennessee and was turned down again. A Tennessee court declared that the election of remedies rule barred the Tennessee claim since the employee had "affirmatively acted" to get benefits in another state. Just because that other state denied his claim, the employee could not then seek the benefits in Tennessee. He had made his choice (Maryland) and to allow a second choice (or a third or fourth) would be unfair to the workers compensation system and a burden to the legal system.

There is another point to consider: the insurer has agreed to pay the benefits required by the *workers compensation law*, a phrase defined on the policy as the "workers compensation law...of each state or territory named in Item 3.A. of the information page." This makes it important for the insured employer to specifically list those states in which the employer has a workers compensation exposure. If, in the example above, the employer did not list Pennsylvania in Item 3.A. of the information page, payment for any benefits won by the claimant employee could be denied by the insurer since Pennsylvania was not a listed state. Of course, Other States Insurance (discussed in Chapter 4) can alleviate this potential problem. But an insured who has workers compensation exposures in more than one state should make sure those states are listed either in Item 3.A. or Item 3.C. of the information page.

## We Will Defend

With this clause, the insurer promises to defend, at its expense, any claim, proceeding, or suit against the insured for benefits payable by the workers compensation policy. It should be noted that the insurer reserves the right to settle claims or lawsuits, so the insured has no veto power over the matter. For example, if the insured does not want to pay benefits to an injured employee because the insured believes the employee is faking the injury, the insurer need not get the permission of the insured in order to pay the claim if it so decides. This is analogous to the duty to defend language in the commercial general liability policy.

In this clause, the insurer also states clearly that it has no duty to defend a claim or lawsuit that is not covered under the terms of the policy. This is for those courts that would say that if a clear denial of the duty to defend under certain circumstances is not placed in the policy language, then the insurer must defend any and all claims or lawsuits.

## We Will Also Pay

The insurer will pay certain enumerated costs as part of any claim, proceeding, or lawsuit that is defended. The listed costs are: reasonable expenses incurred at the insurer's request (but not loss of earnings); premiums for bonds to release attachments and for appeal bonds; litigation costs taxed against the insured; interest on a judgment as required by law; and expenses incurred by the insurer.

These payments are similar to the supplementary payments that are offered under a CGL coverage form. The payments are in addition to the amounts payable as workers compensation payments, so any of these costs that are paid by the insurer will not diminish the amounts available for workers compensation benefits.

## Other Insurance

With this clause, the insurer declares that it will not pay more than its share of benefits and costs covered by the workers compensation policy and other insurance, including self-insurance. The sharing is to be on an equal basis until the loss is paid. Since the benefits paid under workers compensation are set by state law and not subject to the vagaries of a jury, there is no specified limit of liability on the workers compensation policy; however, any amounts to be paid as benefits will be split equally among affected insurers and self-insureds.

## Payments You Must Make

This clause of the workers compensation coverage details when the insured, instead of the insurer, has to make payments arising out of an injured worker's claim. Here the policy points out that the insured is responsible for any payments in excess of the benefits regularly provided by the workers compensation law.

This excess is usually the result of the insured's violating workers compensation laws, such as: serious and willful misconduct, knowingly employing someone in violation of law, failure to comply with a health or safety law, or discharging or discriminating against any employee in violation of law. As an example, if the insured knowingly hires a minor in violation of state workers compensation laws and the minor is injured on the job, the insured will be charged a penalty by the state. The insurer will pay the benefits due the injured worker, but the insured is responsible for the penalty levied by the state. This is an attempt by the insurer to make the insured pay for his or her own intentional conduct that violates a law or regulation, something akin to the expected or intended injury exclusion on the CGL form.

Note that if the insurer makes any of these excess payments on behalf of the insured, the insured must reimburse the insurer promptly. There is no explanation on the policy as to just what "promptly" means, but it is unlikely that an insurer would allow payments due to languish over any length of time.

## Recovery from Others

This is basically a subrogation clause. It entitles the insurer to recover its workers compensation payments from a party that can be shown to be actually liable for an employee's injuries. The insured has the duty to do everything necessary to protect the rights of the insurer and to help enforce those rights. So, for example, if a customer of the insured is somehow responsible for injuries suffered by the insured's employee, the insured is not supposed to waive the right of recovery in an attempt to keep the customer happy. Such a course of action would violate the insurer's rights and lead to a possible dispute over coverage between the insured and the insurer.

This clause does not speak to pre-injury waivers. Therefore, it must be concluded that if the insured has agreements with his or her customers that hold the customers harmless for injuries that may be suffered by the insured's employees arising out of the customers' negligence (an unlikely circumstance), such agreements do not violate the provisions of this clause.

## Statutory Provisions

Where required by law, workers compensation insurance is subject to several statutory provisions. These clauses provide that: notice to the insured of an injury constitutes notice to the insurer; default, bankruptcy, or insolvency of the insured does not relieve the insurer of obligations under the policy (indeed, the insurer states that it is directly and primarily liable to any person entitled to payable benefits); jurisdiction over the insured is jurisdiction over the insurer for purposes of the workers compensation law—that is, the state law that decides if and what compensation is to be paid to the injured employee is the guide for both the insured and the insurer.

The statutory provisions also note that terms of the insurance coverage that conflict with the workers compensation law are changed to conform to the law. In other words, state law takes precedence over the wording of the insurance policy. Workers compensation coverage is guided by state law, not by an insurance policy and not by federal law.

# Chapter 3

# Employers Liability Insurance

Employers liability insurance is the second part of coverage contained in the standard workers compensation policy. It protects the insured against liability imposed by law for injury to employees in the course of employment that is not compensable as an obligation imposed by workers compensation, occupational disease, or any similar laws. The coverage under this part of the workers compensation policy corresponds to liability coverage found on other forms.

Despite the fact that workers compensation is usually considered to be the exclusive remedy for covered employees for work-related injuries, there are several reasons why employers liability coverage is desirable.

Some states do not make workers compensation insurance compulsory or do not require the statutory coverage unless an employer has three or more employees. In either of these circumstances, workers compensation insurance is elective. There may also be instances when an on-the-job injury or disease is not considered to be work-related and therefore not compensable under the statutory coverage. Nevertheless, the employee may still have reason to believe that the employer should be held accountable, and proceed with legal action. Additionally, the workers compensation laws of some states have been interpreted as permitting lawsuits and recovery against employers by spouses and dependents of injured workers, even though the workers are compensated for their injuries. The basis of such lawsuits is loss of consortium—loss of companionship, comfort, and affection.

Finally, employers are increasingly being confronted with claims and lawsuits in so-called *third-party-over* actions; these arise when an injured employee sues a negligent third party who in turn, sues the employer for contributory negligence. For example, a third-party-over action might arise in the following circumstance: a store clerk's eye is injured by an exploding soda bottle cap. The employee sues the soda bottling company (because the judgment would probably exceed workers compensation benefits). The bottler joins the employer in the suit, claiming negligent storage of the bottles. This is a third-party-over action.

Under such circumstances as these, the employer can look to employers liability insurance for coverage.

The employers liability insurance part of the policy contains nine clauses.

## How This Insurance Applies

Employers liability insurance applies to bodily injury by accident or by disease. The bodily injury must arise out of and in the course of employment, and the employment must be necessary or incidental to the named insured's work in a state or territory listed in Item 3.A. of the information page. The same issues regarding the naming of states in 3.A. that apply to workers compensation insurance apply here; see Chapter 1 for comment.

## The Course of Employment

One of the crucial elements of this insurance coverage is the phrase "out of and in the course of employment." The various states' workers compensation laws do not offer a definition of the phrase and neither does the insurance policy. So, it has fallen to the courts to define the phrase; the following court decisions serve as examples.

The Ohio Supreme Court in *Bralley v. Daugherty*, 401 N.E. 2d 448 (Ohio 1980), declared that the "test of the right to participate in the workers compensation fund is...whether a causal connection existed between an employee's injury and his employment." In *Appeal of Griffin*, 671 A.2d 541 (N.H. 1996), the New Hampshire Supreme Court decided that an injury due to a fight with coworkers was employment related. In *Copeland v. Boots Pharmaceuticals,* 916 P.2d 277 (Okla. App. Cts. 1996) an appeals court in Oklahoma found that a traveling sales rep was not injured in an employment related incident when she was bitten by a spider while spending the night in a hotel during a business trip. The key issue in these cases for the courts was whether the employment caused the injury — whether the injury arose out of a personal risk or a business risk. There is a minority judicial opinion in the country that declares that mere presence at the workplace is enough if the employee would not have been injured otherwise; however, an overwhelming majority of state courts require the causal connection if an injury is to be covered by workers compensation and employers liability insurance.

Other important elements in this coverage are: the bodily injury must occur during the policy period; and, if the named insured is sued, the original lawsuit and any related legal actions for damages must be brought in the United States, its territories or possessions, or Canada. These are fairly standard coverage conditions in an insurance policy.

## We Will Pay

Under employers liability insurance, the insurer promises to pay all sums that the insured legally must pay as damages because of bodily injury to employees. The covered damages, where recovery is permitted by law, include: (1) the insured's liability for damages claimed against a third party by one of the insured's employees (third-party-over actions); (2) damages assessed for care and loss of services; and (3) consequential bodily injury to a spouse, child, parent, or sibling of the injured employee. In addition, the employers liability insurance applies to damages assessed against the insured in a capacity other than as an employer (a dual capacity action).

Note that the language of the employers liability coverage complements the language of the workers compensation exclusions that are on the commercial general liability (CGL) form. The covered damages under employers liability correspond well with the damages excluded under the CGL form. As examples: the CGL form excludes coverage for bodily injury to an employee of the insured (or to an employee's spouse, child, parent, brother, or sister for consequential bodily injury) that arises out of and in the course of employment by the insured; the CGL form's exclusions apply whether the insured may be liable either as an employer or in any other capacity (dual capacity); and the exclusions apply if the insured has an obligation to share damages with or repay someone else who must pay damages (third-party-over actions). This is in keeping with the idea that employee injuries should be covered by workers compensation policies and not general liability policies.

## Employers Liability Exclusions

Employers liability coverage is subject to twelve exclusions that highlight the nature of this coverage.

For example, there are exclusions making the point that this policy is meant to apply under state laws and not federal laws. The insurance does not cover bodily injury to any person subject to the Longshore and Harbor Workers Compensation Act, the Defense Base Act, the Federal Coal Mine Health and Safety Act, or any other federal workers compensation law. Bodily injury to any person in work that is subject to the Federal Employers' Liability Act or any other federal laws obligating an employer to pay damages to an employee due to bodily injury arising out of or in the course of employment is also excluded. And, damages payable under the Migrant and Seasonal Agricultural Worker Protection Act and under any other federal law awarding damages for violation of those laws or regulations are excluded.

Other exclusions apply to intentional acts and violations of laws, showing that this coverage is meant for accidental incidents. Employers liability insurance does not cover liability assumed under a contract (note that liability assumed by the insured under an insured contract is covered by the CGL form—another example of one coverage form complementing the other). Employers liability insurance does not cover fines or penalties imposed for violation of federal or state law. It does not cover punitive or exemplary damages because of bodily injury to an employee who is employed in violation of law. And, the insurance does not cover the bodily injury to an employee while employed in violation of law with the actual knowledge of the named insured or any executive officers. This can act as a dual sword of punishment to an insured. For example, if the insured knowingly violates state law and hires a minor for hazardous work and the minor is injured on the job, the insured will no doubt be hit with fines and be sued by the injured minor for compensatory and punitive damages. When that happens, the employers liability insurance will not be applicable for the insured and the insured will carry the monetary burden.

There is an exclusion that applies to damages arising out of coercion, criticism, demotion, evaluation, reassignment, discipline, defamation, harassment, humiliation, discrimination against or termination of any employee, or any personnel practices, policies, acts, or omissions. This multi-worded exclusion emphasizes the point that employers liability insurance is meant for bodily injury suffered by an employee by accident or by disease, and not for mental stress or embarrassment or for something other than bodily injury arising out of a personnel practice or company policy. Even if a court were to equate the mental stress or anxiety of a demotion or harassment with bodily injury, this exclusion is so worded that the policy will not provide employers liability coverage—any "damages" arising out of the listed actions are not covered.

Finally, the policy has an exclusion for bodily injury occurring outside the United States, its territories or possessions, and Canada. This exclusion could pose a huge problem in today's business world since many companies do business on an international scale. However, the exclusion has an exception for bodily injury to a citizen or resident of the U.S. or Canada who is temporarily outside these countries. So, if an employee of the named insured company is in Japan on a business trip and is injured while on the job, employers liability insurance is available to the insured if needed.

## We Will Defend

The policy gives the insurer the right and duty to defend the insured against any claim, proceeding, or lawsuit for damages payable by the employers liability insurance. The insurer reserves the right to settle the claims and lawsuits, so the insured has no veto power over the matter. The defense of the insured is at the expense of the insurer, so the costs of defense do not impact on the declared limits of insurance.

This defense clause adds the stipulations that the insurer has no duty to defend a claim or lawsuit that is not covered by the insurance, and no duty to defend or continue defending after the applicable limit of liability is paid. The purpose of the first caveat is to counter the idea put forth by some courts that unless the insurer specifically declares that it has no duty to defend under certain circumstances, the insurer has to defend the insured under all circumstances, even if there is no coverage under the terms of the policy. The purpose of the second caveat is to keep insurers from continuing to spend money on the defense of the insured after the limits of liability are paid. Now, whether this means that the insurer can simply put the limits of liability into a fund before trial and then walk away from the defense of the insured, is not clear; however, the thinking of most courts today is that such a practice is not acceptable, legally or morally.

## We Will Also Pay

This provision is the same as that found under part one of the workers compensation policy, discussed in Chapter 2. The payments promised here by the insurer are similar to the supplementary payments that are offered under the CGL coverage form, and do not diminish the limits of liability as shown on the information page.

## Other Insurance

This provision is similar to the other insurance clause found under part one of the policy. A discussion of the clause is in Chapter 2.

## Limits of Liability

The insurer's liability to pay for damages is limited. The limits of liability are shown on the information page and are listed as follows: an amount per each accident is listed for bodily injury by accident; a policy limit is listed for bodily injury by disease; and an amount per each employee is listed for bodily injury by disease. This listing of specific limits of liability is, of course, a different approach than the payment schedule under part one of the policy; payments under part one of the policy are guided by the state workers compensation law and not the policy itself. Employers liability is more like a commercial general liability policy, in this regard.

The "by accident" limit is based on each accident so that the insurer will pay no more than the listed amount in any one accident regardless of how many employees are injured. For example, if three employees are injured in the same accident and the bodily injury by accident limit is $100,000, then that is the total amount payable by the insurer. This is not to say that all three employees will receive equal amounts—that is to be decided by the facts of the case—but, they will receive a total of $100,000.

The "by disease" limit has an aggregate limit and an each employee limit. The aggregate limit shown on the information page is the total amount payable by the insurer for all bodily injuries arising out of a disease, regardless of the number of employees who suffer injury from the disease. So, for example, if thirty employees suffer injury from a disease for which the employer is legally liable, the total amount available for all the injured employees is the amount listed as the policy limit for bodily injury by disease. How the amount is split up is decided by the facts of the case. The disease limit is also subject to an each employee limit in that, regardless of the aggregate limit, each employee injured by disease can collect only up to the amount listed on the information page.

As an example, the insured has a $250,000 policy limit for injury by disease and a $25,000 limit for each employee for injury by disease. If the thirty employees noted in the previous paragraph are injured by disease, they have a $250,000 pool to be divided among them, but each employee can only be paid under this policy a total of $25,000. These scheduled limits of liability may not be enough to completely pay the amounts for which the insured is found liable, but scheduled limits of liability are legal and not very likely to be disregarded by courts.

The standard limit of liability under employers liability insurance for bodily injury by accident is $100,000 per each accident. The standard limit for bodily injury by disease is $100,000 per employee, with a per policy aggregate of $500,000. Increased limits are available for an additional premium.

## Recovery from Others

This is the subrogation clause for employers liability insurance. It is similar to the clause in the workers compensation insurance part of the policy which is discussed in Chapter 2.

## Actions Against Us

This provision spells out a bit of the contractual relationship between the insured and the insurer. The insured has agreed not to exercise a right of action; that is, file a lawsuit, against the insurer unless certain things have occurred. Basically, the insured agrees not to sue the insurer unless a claim has been filed against the insured, all the provisions of the policy have been followed by the insured, a definite amount of liability has been assessed against the insured, and then, the insurer has, for whatever reason, refused to pay the amount due.

This clause makes the point that the workers compensation policy is a contractual agreement between the insured and the insurer and so, no outside party—one not a party to the contract—has the right under this policy to sue the insurer to enforce the provisions of the policy.

The insurer agrees through this provision not to abandon its contractual commitments under the policy to the insured even if the insured goes bankrupt or becomes insolvent. Existing claims will still be paid even if the insured is no longer in business.

# Chapter 4

# Other States Insurance

This part of the workers compensation and employers liability insurance policy provides *other states insurance*. This coverage functions as a complement to part one of the policy, in that part one (workers compensation insurance) applies to obligations imposed on the insured by the compensation laws of states listed in Item 3.A. of the information page, while other states insurance applies only if a state(s) is shown in Item 3.C. of the information page. This means that if an insured is confronted with a claim under a workers compensation law of a state to which the insured had not fully expected to be subject—a state not listed in Item 3.A. of the declarations—there is no coverage under part one of the policy; but the insured could find coverage for such a claim by utilizing the other states insurance part of the workers compensation policy.

Other states insurance applies if one or more states where the insured reasonably anticipates working in are shown in Item 3.C. of the information page. The insured has no known exposure in those states listed in Item 3.C. when the policy becomes effective, but the insured thinks an exposure may arise (e.g., an employee might travel to one of those states on business or be unexpectedly assigned out-of-state). If the insured begins work in one of the listed states after the effective date of the policy, the policy applies as if that state were listed in Item 3.A. for workers compensation and employers liability purposes. To avoid an uninsured loss due to oversight, it has been suggested that the statement, "All states except North Dakota, Ohio, Washington, West Virginia, Wyoming (monopolistic states) and states designated in Item 3.A. of the information page," be inserted in Item 3.C. However, an insurer licensed to operate in only a limited number of states should not include this broad statement in the workers compensation policy because it might convey to some the impression that the insurer has the ability to write insurance in all states. This is not the case, of course, since other states insurance does not give any insurer the approval to write workers compensation coverage in a particular state if that insurer is not licensed to do so.

A fairly common situation under which the other states insurance is useful is that of an insured firm that can have employees traveling in states other than the state where the firm is located. For example, if the insured has its office in Illinois and all its employees work there, the insured would list Illinois in Item 3.A. of the information page of the policy. Due to new business opportunities, the insured believes that it will have some employees travel into Iowa, Missouri, Indiana, and Wisconsin on business. To properly cover this possible exposure, the insured would list the four states in Item 3.C. of the information page (of course, if the insured thinks its employees would be going to more than the four states named, the insured can use the "all states ..." language noted in the previous paragraph). If the insured does begin any work in those states listed in Item 3.C. after the effective date of the workers compensation policy, the insured would have workers compensation insurance if needed. The insurer agrees to pay the benefits required by the workers compensation law of the listed states, or, if not permitted to pay the benefits directly to the injured employee, the insurer agrees to reimburse the insured for the benefits that it paid the employee.

## Notice Clauses

A key point in this part of the workers compensation policy is the importance of giving notice to the insurer. The policy emphasizes that if the insured already has ongoing work on the effective date of the policy in any state not listed in Item 3.A. of the information page, "Coverage will not be afforded for that state unless we (the insurer) are notified within thirty days." For example, if the insured has employees working in Delaware at the time his workers compensation policy renews, and Delaware is not listed under Item 3.A. of the information page, the insured must notify the insurer of the Delaware exposure within thirty days or there is no coverage for workers compensation claims that may arise after that time period expires.

Note that this thirty day time period is, presumably, thirty days after policy inception, but the policy's wording is not clear on that point. In order for the insured to be safe, the insurer should be notified of work begun in states other than those listed in Item 3.A. as soon as such work begins, and not wait for any thirty day time period to go by. In fact, in support of this immediate notice idea, the policy has another paragraph that reminds the insured to, "Tell us (the insurer) at once if you begin work in any state listed in Item 3.C. of the information page." Through these measures, the insurer is simply trying to exercise a degree of control over the loss potential.

# Chapter 5

# Duties After Injury Occurs/Conditions

This chapter deals with parts four and six of the workers compensation and employers liability insurance policy. Part four of the policy sets out the duties that the named insured must perform if an injury occurs lest the insured breach contractual obligations, thereby making the insurance contract voidable. Part six discusses certain conditions that affect the policy and some of the actions of the insured and the insurer in their dealings with one another.

## The Duties of the Insured

The policy lists seven duties that the insured is to undertake in the event of an injury occurring to an employee.

First and foremost is the duty to notify the insurer if an injury that may be covered by the policy occurs. The obvious reason for this is so that the insurer can process an injury claim promptly. Such promptness can aid the insured, the insurer, and the injured employee. With prompt notice, the insured gets the ball rolling so that the insurance coverage he has already paid for can be applied to the claim. The injured worker gets quick appropriate medical attention and care, knowing that such care is going to be paid for by the insurer. The insurer can set up its claim file and fulfill its contractual obligations to "pay promptly when due" the workers compensation benefits required by law; and, if a lawsuit results from the injury, prompt notice allows the insurer to have the facts and figures of the injury incident so that a defense can be planned or a subrogation lawsuit can be successfully made. It is true that some insureds may want to hide a worker's injury in order to protect its experience rating factor, but that would not only violate the insured's duties under the policy contract, but also set the stage for possible future problems in the insurer-insured-employee relationship.

The next listed duty of the insured is to provide for immediate medical and other services required by the workers compensation law. This may conflict with the duty noted in the last paragraph of this part of the policy. That last paragraph warns the insured not to voluntarily make payments, assume obligations, or incur expenses, except at the insured's own cost. If, in the process of providing immediate medical services, the insured incurs expenses, are such expenses reimbursable by the insurer? The policy is not clear on this point; however, in all probability, the insured will be reimbursed. Note that the insurer has already promised to pay reasonable expenses incurred by the insured at its request, and since the insurer has "requested" the insured to provide immediate medical services if an injury occurs, it can be said that the insurer has already agreed to the reimbursement. Besides, the duty of the insured is to not voluntarily make payments or incur expenses; but, if the immediate medical services are required by law, that is not exactly voluntary on the part of the insured.

If an injury occurs, the insured must give the insurer or the agent the names and addresses of the injured persons and of witnesses, and other information needed by the insurer. And, the insured is required to promptly give the insurer all notices, demands, and legal papers related to the injury, claim, or lawsuit. This helps the insurer to process the claim as soon as possible, and to plan for any future legal action on behalf of or against the insured.

The insured has the duty to cooperate with the insurer and to assist in the investigation, settlement, or defense of any claim, proceeding, or lawsuit. This is not to say that the insured has the final say in any settlement; the insurer has already reserved to itself that task. But, the insured has an affirmative duty to cooperate with the insurer in the claims process, and most courts would require the insured to fulfill this duty or be held in breach of contract.

The final listed duty of the insured deals with the insurer's right of subrogation. The insured must do nothing after an injury occurs that would interfere with the insurer's right to recover from others. The duty says nothing about an insured signing a waiver or some other type of hold harmless agreement prior to an injury that would restrict or even deny a right to recover from others, so such agreements would apply to the insurer as well as to the insured. Insureds should make such agreements known to the insurer before the policy takes effect.

Note again, if the insured violates these duties, there is the chance that the insurer will claim breach of contract, thus making the policy voidable. The insurer would have to prove such a breach, but if it can do so the insured could end up with no insurance coverage for a workers compensation claim.

## Conditions

There are five conditions listed on the workers compensation policy, dealing with inspections, long term policies, the transfer of the named insured's rights, cancellation of the policy, and just who acts as the sole representative on behalf of all the insureds.

The inspections clause gives the insurer the right to make an inspection of the workplace "at any time." This condition has given rise to a theory that would allow the injured employee to maintain an action for negligence against the workers compensation insurance carier itself. The reasoning behind this is that some insurance carriers take it upon themselves to inspect the workplace for safety engineering purposes, and if an accident then occurs, the injured worker can charge negligence on the part of the insurer for failure to perform its assumed duty to uncover and correct unsafe working conditions.

To date, most judicial decisions in this area have come down on the side of the insurer. A federal district court in Michigan stated in *Kotarski v. Aetna Casualty & Surety Company*, 244 F.Supp. 547 (E.D. Mich. 1965) that nothing in Michigan's workers compensation act reveals the intention to allow the insurer that is performing safety inspections as an integral part of its business function to be sued as a negligent third party on the theory that its liability arises from negligent performance of a voluntary undertaking. In *Barrette v. Travelers Insurance Company*, 246 A.2d 102 (Conn. Super. Ct. 1968), the Connecticut Supreme Court decided that an employer's compensation carrier is not subject to suit by an injured employee for alleged negligence in the failure to inspect machinery, failure to warn the employee of the danger, or neglecting to provide devices to negate the danger. Also, in *Reid v. Employers Mutual Liability Insurance Company*, 319 N.E.2d 769 (Ill. 1974), the Illinois Supreme Court held that the workers compensation insurer engaged in making safety inspections incident to its compensation coverage was not amenable to a lawsuit by an employee for injuries caused by the carrier's negligence in performing safety inspections.

There are, of course, some cases on the other side of the issue. In a New Hampshire case, *Corson v. Liberty Mutual Insurance Company*, 265 A.2d

315 (N.H. 1970), a workers compensation insurer that undertook the task of assisting accident prevention by inspections and advice rendered to the insured employer was liable to an injured employee for a negligent inspection. And, in *Rothfuss v. Bakers Mutual Insurance Company*, 733 A.2d 315 (N.J. Super. Ct. App. Div. 1969), the New Jersey Supreme Court declared that a workers compensation carrier is a third person liable to an employee in a common law action if its acts negligently cause harm to the employee.

Regardless of which side of the argument prevails in any given state, it should be pointed out that the current workers compensation and employers liability insurance policy contains a rather specific disclaimer about the inspection of the workplace and the duty such an inspection places on the insurer. In the inspection condition of the policy, the insurance company declares that inspections it may carry out are not safety inspections; they relate only to the insurability of the workplaces and the premiums to be charged. Furthermore, the insurer states that it does not undertake to perform the duty of any person to provide for the health or safety of the employees, and does not warrant that the workplaces are safe or healthful, or that they comply with laws, codes, or standards. Thus, the insurer strives to intentionally limit its duty under the workers compensation policy to both the insured and the employee.

The long term policy clause notes that, if a policy is written for longer than one year and sixteen days—say, for example, two or three years—then all the provisions in the existing policy apply as if under a brand new policy. In other words, the annual renewal is treated as an automatic rewrite of the existing policy, though both the insured and the insurer should reexamine the exposures in order to get proper premium for proper coverage.

The transfer of rights clause acts to prevent the insured from transferring his or her rights or duties to another party without the written consent of the insurer. This is meant to protect the insurer from getting an insured that it neither contracted for nor would want to insure in any instance. An exception is made, of course, for the legal representative of the insured in case the insured dies; notice must be given to the insurer within thirty days after the insured's death.

The cancellation clause details how the insured or the insurer can cancel the policy. The clause allows the insured to cancel the policy at any time, even with only one day notice, as long as written notice is mailed to the insurance company in advance of the cancellation date. It should be noted that the clause states that notice need only be mailed in advance and not received by the company in advance. If the insurer cancels the policy, it must mail or deliver to the insured not less than ten days advance written notice stating when the cancellation is to take effect. For the insurer also, mailing the notice will prove sufficient to prove notice. Presumably, should any dispute arise over the cancellation date, a court will decide if the terms of the clause were heeded, but regardless of which party is mailing the cancellation notice, it would be prudent to mail it by certified mail, return receipt requested. This clause also states the obvious—if the cancellation provisions conflict with state law, the state law prevails and this policy and the insurer recognize that fact.

The final condition on the policy makes the first named insured the sole representative to the insurer, so that important items such as changing the policy provisions or cancelling the policy can be dealt with without having the insurer sort through possibly conflicting statements or wishes from the various insureds. This is simply a good and sensible business practice.

# Chapter 6

# Endorsements

There are many endorsements authorized for use with the workers compensation and employers liability insurance policy. This chapter lists some of them and analyzes their content. It should be noted that there are state-specific endorsements that are applicable only in that particular state named in the endorsement that bring the policy into conformity with state law or regulation; but, those are too numerous to discuss in this guide. And, there are endorsements that pertain to federal laws on the subject of workers compensation, such as the maritime coverage endorsement and the federal employers liability coverage endorsement. These are discussed in a later chapter.

The endorsements in this chapter are presented in numerical order.

## Alternate Employer Endorsement WC 00 03 01 A

This endorsement applies only with respect to bodily injury to the named insured's employees who are in the course of special or temporary employment by the alternate employer listed on the endorsement. An example of when this endorsement can be used is the following: a supplier of temporary office help (the insured) is required by its customer (the user of the temporary office help, that is, the alternate employer) to provide this insurance to protect the customer from claims brought by the insured's employees against the alternate employer. If the named insured has an employee who is injured while working for the alternate employer listed on the endorsement, WC 00 03 01 A will provide coverage for claims made by the employee against that alternate employer. Of course, the insurance afforded by the endorsement is not intended to satisfy the alternate employer's duty to secure its own obligations under the workers compensation law of the state.

## Employers Liability Coverage Endorsement WC 00 03 03 B

This endorsement is usually used in monopolistic states where the workers compensation system is not open to coverage by private insurance companies. WC 00 03 03 B states up front that part one of the workers compensation policy—workers compensation insurance—does not apply to work in a state shown in the schedule. On the other hand, part two— employers liability insurance—applies to work in the listed states as though the states were shown in Item 3.A. of the information page. Basically, WC 00 03 03 B provides stop gap coverage for employers in those states where the state runs the workers compensation program but does not offer employers liability coverage. Note that in Ohio, endorsement WC 34 03 01 B is used in place of WC 00 03 03 B.

## Joint Venture as Insured Endorsement WC 00 03 05

WC 00 03 05 is fairly straightforward. It states, "If the employer named in Item 1 of the information page is a joint venture, and if you are one of its members, you are insured, but only in your capacity as an employer of the joint venture's employees." The workers compensation policy makes no mention of business arrangements such as joint ventures, but, joint ventures can, of course, be employers. This endorsement makes the point that the insurance afforded by the workers compensation policy is limited to being an employer of those employees that are working for the joint venture. If an employer is involved in a joint venture but also has other business interests and operations, he will need a separate workers compensation policy to apply to injuries suffered by those employees working in the other businesses and operations; WC 00 03 05 will not respond to such claims.

## Medical Benefits Exclusion Endorsement WC 00 03 06

Some states permit insureds to pay medical benefits directly, instead of channeling them through the workers compensation policy. Endorsement WC 00 03 06 is attached in such situations. It states that workers compensation medical benefits of a state listed on the endorsement are not covered. The endorsement directs that the insured pay medical benefits as required by law and to the satisfaction of the insurer.

## Medical Benefits Reimbursement Endorsement WC 00 03 07

This endorsement is similar to WC 00 03 06, discussed previously. It states that the insured will provide medical benefits as required by law in the states listed. The insurer also must be satisfied with the way in which benefits are being paid. In addition, the insured is obligated to reimburse the insurer for any medical benefits that it may legally be required to pay.

## Partners, Officers and Others Exclusion Endorsement WC 00 03 08

Some states allow partners and executive officers to choose to be subject to the workers compensation laws. If these people so choose, the premium basis of the workers compensation policy includes their remuneration. However, where the individual partners or executive officers choose not to be covered by the workers compensation laws, WC 00 03 08 should be attached to the policy. The endorsement states that the policy does not cover bodily injury to any person described in the schedule and that the premium basis for the policy does not include their remuneration. Note that individuals can be named on this endorsement only when the state workers compensation law allows it.

## Sole Proprietors, Partners, Officers and Others Coverage Endorsement WC 00 03 10

In contrast to WC 00 03 08, endorsement WC 00 03 10 is used when partners and executive officers choose to be subject to the workers compensation laws. The endorsement notes that the persons described on the schedule have chosen to be subject to the law and that the premium basis for the policy includes their remuneration. As with the previous endorsement, individuals can be named in this endorsement only when it is allowed by the state workers compensation law.

## Voluntary Compensation and Employers Liability Coverage Endorsement WC 00 03 11

WC 00 03 11 can be used to cover all employees, like domestic or farm workers, who are not subject to the workers compensation laws, and it can be attached to an existing workers compensation policy that is in place for those employees that are required by state law to be covered by the workers compensation system.

Coverage provided under this endorsement is identical to that for employers and employees required to be insured under the law. WC 00 03 11 states that the insurer "will pay an amount equal to the benefits that would be required of you if you and your employees described in the schedule were subject to the workers compensation law shown in the schedule. We will pay those amounts to the persons who would be entitled to them under the law." In other words, benefits are provided for injuries that would have been compensable in the same manner as they would have been provided had the employment been subject to any applicable state workers compensation laws.

The insurance provided by WC 00 03 11 applies to bodily injury sustained by an employee in the group of employees described in the endorsement's schedule. The bodily injury must occur in the course of employment necessary or incidental to work in a state listed in the schedule and must occur during the policy period. The insurance does not cover any obligation imposed by a workers compensation law or bodily injury intentionally caused or aggravated by the named insured.

Note that before any payments are made to those entitled to them, the beneficiaries must release the insured and the insurer, in writing, of all responsibility for the injury. Any right to recover from others who may be responsible for the injury must be transferred to the insurer, and the injured party must cooperate fully with the insurer in enforcing the right of recovery. If the persons entitled to the benefits of the insurance fail to do these things, or if they claim damages from the insured or the insurer, the duty to pay under this endorsement ends at once.

## Voluntary Compensation and Employers Liability Coverage for Residence Employees Endorsement WC 00 03 12

WC 00 03 12 is something of a companion endorsement to WC 00 03 11. Both offer voluntary compensation coverage, but as WC 00 03 11 should be used by corporations and business entities, WC 00 03 12 can be used by homeowners. If a homeowner wants workers compensation coverage for a domestic worker, such as a housekeeper or a gardener, WC 00 03 12 is the fitting manner for coverage.

WC 00 03 12 adds voluntary compensation and employers liability coverage for residence employees to a homeowners policy, a personal liability policy, or some other policy that provides similar personal liability coverage. The insurance applies to bodily injury by accident or disease sustained by the named insured's residence employees and must arise out of and in the course of employment by the named insured. So, an advantage of this coverage is that if a domestic worker who cannot be brought within the workers compensation system due to state law is injured and sues the named insured employer, WC 00 03 12 will provide protection to the named insured.

The insuring agreement, exclusions, and other provisions of WC 00 03 12 are similar to those of WC 00 03 11, but there is an important point to mention. In keeping with the "personal"—as opposed to the "business"—nature of WC 00 03 12, the endorsement has an exclusion that states that coverage does not apply to bodily injury arising out of any of the named insured's business pursuits.

## Waiver of Our Right to Recover from Others Endorsement WC 00 03 13

The insurer, through this endorsement, waives its right of subrogation against third parties who may be responsible for an injury if those third parties are named in the endorsement's schedule.

## Workers Compensation and Employers Liability Coverage for Residence Employees Endorsement WC 00 03 14

In jurisdictions where domestic, agricultural, and casual workers are subject to the state's workers compensation laws, the employer is required to provide coverage. One way to arrange for this coverage is through the use of WC 00 03 14. This endorsement contains basically the same provisions as the standard workers compensation and employers liability policy and is to be attached to a personal liability policy, a homeowners policy, or any policy affording similar personal liability coverage with respect to the residence premises of the insured. The effect is the same as if the employee were covered by a standard workers compensation policy since the insurer agrees to pay benefits required by the state's workers compensation laws.

## Domestic and Agricultural Workers Exclusion Endorsement WC 00 03 15

Domestic, agricultural, and casual employees are not treated in a uniform manner under the workers compensation systems of the various states. Some states have written their workers compensation laws to include domestic and agricultural employees either on a compulsory basis, or to allow employees to provide coverage voluntarily. WC 00 03 15 can be used by insureds to deny workers compensation benefits coverage to any agricultural, domestic, or household worker as long as the state law allows this course of action. Those workers denied coverage have to be listed in the endorsement's schedule.

## Employee Leasing Client Endorsement WC 00 03 19

This endorsement is attached to policies issued to labor contracting businesses. It specifies that coverage for leased workers will be provided by the business that is leasing the employees under contract (the client), not the labor contractor. The endorsement requires that the labor contractor provide its insurer with the following information within thirty days of entering a labor contract: contract effective date and term; client's name; client's federal employer identification number; client's mailing address; and number of workers leased, description of duties of each, and work location for each. Clients of the labor contract must maintain workers compensation coverage for their direct and leased workers, and proof of that coverage must be submitted to the labor contractor's insurer. If proof is not submitted, the labor contractor must pay premium for the leased employees and the insurer may cancel the labor contractor's policy.

## Labor Contractor Endorsement WC 00 03 20 A

This endorsement is attached to the policy issued to businesses that lease workers—*the client*—from a labor contracting business. It specifies that leased employees will be covered for workers compensation under the client's insurance policy. It is used in conjunction with WC 00 03 19, which is attached to the labor contractor's policy. If the client's insurer is not permitted to pay benefits directly, the insurer will reimburse the labor contractor for benefits it is required to pay for the leased employees. This endorsement does not satisfy the labor contractor's need to carry workers compensation coverage. It addresses only the employees leased by the client from the labor contractor specified in the schedule for the states listed. The coverage may be further restricted to a specific contract or project on which the leased employees are working.

## Labor Contractor Exclusion Endorsement WC 00 03 21

This endorsement defines employee leasing as an arrangement in which a business engages a third party to provide it with workers for a fee or other compensation. The third party is referred to as the *labor contractor*. The entity leasing the employees is called the *client*. The endorsement excludes coverage for workers that the labor contractor leases to clients listed on the endorsement. Coverage must be provided by the client. The endorsement is attached to a labor contractor's policy. Temporary workers are not considered leased workers.

## Employee Leasing Client Exclusion
## Endorsement WC 00 03 22

This endorsement limits coverage under the policy to employees of the insured who are not leased from third parties; it excludes coverage under the policy for workers that the insured leases from labor contractors. It defines labor contractor and client in the same way as does WC 00 03 21.

## Anniversary Rating Date Endorsement WC 00 04 02

As discussed in Chapter 10, most companies are subject to experience rating. The experience modification is subject to change on the anniversary rating date of the company, which usually corresponds with the inception date of the policy. However, there are times when the anniversary rating date differs from the policy inception date. When this happens, WC 00 04 02 is attached. The endorsement states that the premium, rates, and experience modification used on the policy may be changed at the anniversary rating date that is shown in the endorsement.

## Experience Rating Modification Factor
## Endorsement WC 00 04 03

This endorsement is attached when the experience modification that applies to the policy is not available when it is issued. WC 00 04 03 states that the factor will be endorsed onto the policy when it becomes available. The premium is subject to change if the modification differs from the one used to issue the policy.

## Premium Discount Endorsement
## WC 00 04 06 or WC 00 04 06 A

Chapter 9 includes a discussion of the premium discount. Endorsements WC 00 04 06 and WC 00 04 06 A may be used to outline the premium discount percentages that apply to the ascending premium amount.

## Retrospective Premium Endorsement
## One Year Plan WC 00 05 03 A

This endorsement acknowledges that a one-year retrospective rating plan is in effect. The endorsement outlines the retrospective premium formula and program elements, including the policies subject to retro rating; loss limitation, if any; loss conversion factor; minimum and maximum premium factors; basic premium factors; and the tax multipliers, excess loss premium factors, and retrospective development factors as they apply in the states where retrospective rating is applicable. Additional information on how retrospective rating works is provided in Chapter 11.

## Retrospective Premium Endorsement
## Three Year Plan WC 00 05 04 A

This is similar to endorsement WC 00 05 03 A, but it pertains to a three-year retro program.

## Retrospective Premium Endorsement
## One Year Plan—Multiple Lines WC 00 05 12 A

This endorsement is used when a one-year retrospective rating plan applies to multiple lines of insurance, such as workers compensation and employers liability, general liability, and auto liability. It lists the same items that are included in WC 00 05 03 A for all policies that are included in the retrospective rating program.

## Retrospective Premium Endorsement
## Three Year Plan—Multiple Lines WC 00 05 13 A

This is similar to endorsement WC 00 05 12 A, but it pertains to a three-year retro program that covers more than one line of insurance.

## Benefits Deductible Endorsement WC 00 06 03

Some states permit a deductible to be applied to medical, indemnity (wage loss), or medical and indemnity benefits. Endorsement WC 00 06 03 is used to list the deductibles for each type of benefit, as well as the states in which they apply. The deductible amounts apply separately to each claim for bodily injury by accident or disease, unless state law requires payment on a per accident or per disease basis. If the second case applies, the deductibles are applied separately to each accident or disease, regardless of how many employees are injured in the respective accident or by the disease.

The endorsement also specifies that the insurance company will pay the deductible amount for the insured. The policy may be canceled if the insured does not reimburse the carrier for deductible amounts paid within thirty days of a billing notice. In jurisdictions where the insured is permitted to directly pay the deductible, the insurance company becomes the guarantor for the payments.

# Chapter 7

# Nonprivate Insurance

## Monopolistic State Funds

One area of workers compensation insurance that can be a source of confusion concerns the procedures employers with interstate operations must follow when coverage is necessary in states that have monopolistic state funds. There are five such states in this category: North Dakota, Ohio, Washington, West Virginia, and Wyoming. Note that Nevada dropped its monopolistic status effective July 1, 1999.

The discussion that follows concerns these five states. It outlines, in summary form and on a state-by-state basis, some of the procedures that must be followed in determining whether workers compensation needs to be purchased, and if such insurance is required, how to go about purchasing it.

## North Dakota

The Workforce Safety & Insurance Fund administers the insurance under the act in North Dakota. The address of the bureau is: Workforce Safety & Insurance, 1600 E. Century Avenue, Suite 1, Bismarck, ND 58503; (701) 328-3800; Fax: (701) 328-3750.

All public employees and most employees (one or more) within the categories of private or hazardous employments are classified as compulsory under the workers compensation act of this state.

Employers exempt from the act are those who employ farm labor, domestic servants, and casual workers. Nonhazardous employments and employers, including officers of a business corporation, excepted from the compulsory provisions of the act are eligible however, for coverage on a voluntary basis. If an employer in this situation does not wish to purchase insurance, it still retains its common law defenses, but is vulnerable to judgments that might exceed the state's specified workers compensation benefits.

North Dakota has reciprocal agreements with a number of states which have the effect of exempting nonresident employees who are covered by workers compensation insurance in their home state from the provisions of the North Dakota act while temporarily within this state. This extraterritorial provision, however, does not apply to resident employees of North Dakota.

Those states that have reciprocal agreements with North Dakota are: Colorado, Idaho, Montana, Nevada, Oregon, South Dakota, Utah, Washington, and Wyoming. Employees from all other states must be covered by workers compensation insurance from the North Dakota fund.

When a firm desires workers compensation insurance in the state of North Dakota for out-of-state employees, it can either write or call the bureau giving an estimate of its expected payroll in that state and describing the type of work to be performed. The bureau will then inform the employer about the cost of insurance per classification and about the total advance premium necessary to deposit prior to the commencement of work in North Dakota.

When such a request involves a subcontractor, a certificate of insurance is issued for the prime contractor. The bureau also submits a copy of this certificate to the secretary of state indicating that the subcontractor is in good standing with the workers compensation bureau. The subcontractor is then in a position to request a contractor's license from the secretary of state thereby enabling him to commence work in North Dakota.

## Ohio

In Ohio, the Bureau of Workers Compensation and the Industrial Commission administer the state insurance fund. Both agencies are governed by chapters 4121 and 4123 of the Ohio Revised Code. The address for the bureau is: Ohio Bureau of Workers Compensation, 30 W. Spring Street, Columbus, Ohio 43215; (614) 466-2950; Fax: (877) 520-6446.

The bureau is the administrative branch of the Ohio system of workers compensation. Its responsibility is to process all claims, keep account records, conduct audits, and to collect premiums from employers, among other duties.

The Industrial Commission is the adjudicative branch of the Ohio system. It hears and decides all contested claims, determines total and permanent disability, approves premium rates calculated and recommended by the bureau of workers compensation, and determines manual classifications.

All employers of one or more full or part time employees must either purchase insurance from the fund or qualify as self-insurers. Also subject to the law, on a compulsory basis, are employers of domestic workers who earn $160 or more in cash from a single household in any calendar quarter.

The act is also compulsory for state, county, city, township, and incorporated village officials, as well as school districts.

If an employer is a partnership or a sole proprietor, the employer may elect to include, as employees, any members of such partnership or the owner of the sole proprietorship. It is important to note, however, that the employer must provide written notice naming the persons to be covered. No partner or proprietor is considered an employee until such notice is made and acknowledged.

Nonresident employees who are covered by workers compensation insurance in their own state are exempt from the provisions of the Ohio act for a maximum period of ninety days. After that period, the employer must purchase insurance for its employees from the Ohio fund. However, any nonresident employer who hires employees from within the state of Ohio for work in that state must purchase coverage from the Ohio fund.

When an employer desires workers compensation insurance in the state of Ohio, it must request an application (form U-3) from the underwriting section of the bureau or from any one of its sixteen district offices.

To insure proper handling of its account, an employer must be sure its application adequately describes the operation for proper classification. The employer must also report its payroll according to the correct classification. The coverage is effective on the business day that the employer's check *is received* by the bureau.

When coverage begins, the employer must make an estimate of payroll for eight months. The bureau will then apply the rate to the estimate and bill the employer for that amount. This advance deposit insures coverage during the six month period plus the two month grace period for reporting actual premiums. The state insurance fund manual, which contains a description of each classification, rates for each classification, and rules governing risks, is published annually by the bureau and is available to employers upon request.

The bureau operates on a fiscal year of July 1 to June 30 for premium purposes. In June and December of each year, the bureau sends out payroll reports to be completed by employers. Payroll reports are due on January 31 and July 31. Coverage lapses if premiums are not paid by March 1 and September 1.

## Washington

The state agency that administers the workers compensation insurance program in Washington is the Department of Labor and Industries. The address for the agency is: Department of Labor and Industries, Industrial Insurance Division, P.O. Box 4400, Olympia, Washington 98504-4000; (360) 902-5800; Fax: (360) 902-5798.

Almost all employees must be covered by workers compensation insurance. Those exempt from the act are: sole proprietors and partners; corporate officers; casual employees not connected with a trade, profession or business; domestic servants—unless two or more are regularly employed 40 or more hours a week; and any person employed to do maintenance, repair, remodeling or similar work in or about the private home of the employer, provided the work does not exceed ten consecutive work days.

Also exempt are: persons performing services in return for aid or sustenance from any religious or charitable organization; an employee subject to either the Longshore and Harbor Workers Act or the Jones Act; law enforcement officers and fire fighters hired prior to October 1, 1977; minor children under eighteen years of age on a family farm; musicians and entertainers; and insurance brokers or salesmen.

Self-insurance is permitted if an employer can meet certain qualifications. Self-insuring employers must show their financial ability by providing a surety bond or a deposit equal to an amount that is calculated annually by the Department of Labor and Industries. Such employers must also establish their own safety organizations to provide service similar to that provided by the safety division of the department. Furthermore, these firms must have been in business for three years and have a net minimum worth of $5 million.

Employers that have employees who are not residents of Washington may be exempt from the workers compensation law of Washington if work is of a temporary nature and this state has a reciprocal agreement with the home state of such employee. In these cases, employers are required to submit a certificate to the Department of Labor and Industries stating to the effect that employees will be working in the state of Washington for a period of time and that they are covered under the workers compensation act of their home state.

Those states that have reciprocal agreements with Washington are: Idaho, Montana, Nevada, North Dakota, South Dakota, Oregon, and Wyoming. Employees of all other states must be covered under the workers compensation act of Washington, assuming the type of work being performed is not exempt from the law.

In order to apply for workers compensation insurance in the state of Washington, an employer must request an application from the department or any one of its fifteen district offices. This "master business application" will open accounts with five agencies in Washington, thus avoiding multiple applications. Classification is made according to the business that the firm is engaged in and not by individual employments.

Two premiums are charged for coverage and there is one assessment: (1) the industrial insurance premium; (2) the medical aid premium; and (3) the supplemental pension fund assessment.

The industrial insurance premium is paid entirely by the employer. This rate is assessed according to the number of workers hours and premiums are paid quarterly. The medical aid premium is shared equally by the employer and employee. Both premiums are experience rated after three years. Also shared equally is the assessment for the pension fund.

After coverage is written by the department, the employer must complete quarterly reports of payroll. These become due thirty days following the end of the quarter that is being reported.

## West Virginia

In West Virginia, the workers compensation fund is administered by BrickStreet Mutual Insurance Company . The address is: BrickStreet Mutual Insurance Company; 4700 MacCorkle Avenue; Charleston, West Virginia 25304-1964; (304) 926-3400; Fax: (304) 924-5372. This transition to a private company took effect January 1, 2006. BrickStreet will be the sole source of workers' compensation coverage for all employers in West Virginia until July 1, 2008, when the insurance market will open to all private carriers licensed to conduct business in West Virginia. Through 2012, BrickStreet will continue to be the sole source of workers' compensation coverage for state agencies, boards, commissions and higher education.

Workers compensation in West Virginia is compulsory for all firms, associations, and corporations which regularly employ any person for purposes of carrying on any form of industry, service, or business in that state, except the following: employers of domestic workers; employers of five or fewer full time employees in agriculture; employers of employees that are employed outside of the state except in cases of temporary employment; employers of three or fewer temporary or intermittent workers whose period of employment does not exceed ten calendar days in a quarter; employers that are churches; employers engaged in organized professional sports activities; and employers of those who are officers of and stockholders in an S-corporation. However, any of the excepted categories may elect coverage, as may members of partnerships and self-employed persons.

Although workers compensation insurance is compulsory in this state, there are no restrictions or prerequisites for an out-of-state employer who may hire nonresidents to work in West Virginia. Whenever there is a possibility of conflict of workers compensation laws as to any employer in good standing with the West Virginia workers compensation fund because contracted for work may be performed in another state, the parties may agree in writing to be bound by the law of either state if the agreement is filed within ten days with the commissioner. If the parties to coverage agree to be bound by the law of West Virginia, an injured employee will be entitled to the benefits of that state regardless of where injury might occur, that is, inside or outside the state of West Virginia. However, if the parties agree to be bound by the workers compensation law of some other state and the employer is in compliance with the law of that state at the time of injury, the law of that state detailing the benefits and rights of the employee and his dependents shall represent the exclusive remedy against the employer, regardless of where the injury ultimately occurs.

If an out-of-state employer elects to come within the act, it must first furnish the commissioner with a certified copy of a certificate from the secretary of state of West Virginia, authorizing such employer to conduct business in this state. The proper form and information can be obtained from the office of the Secretary of State, Capitol Building, Charleston, West Virginia 25305.

Next, an employer must, in becoming a subscriber to the compensation fund, execute an election agreement and make a deposit equal to the first quarter's estimated premium payment. The minimum quarterly premium is ten dollars. After these are received, the employer relations division assigns the classes and rates corresponding to the employer's operation in West Virginia.

# Wyoming

In the state of Wyoming, workers compensation coverage is compulsory only for specifically required industries or occupations. The Workers' Safety and Compensation Division administers the state fund. The address is: Department of Employment, Workers' Safety and Compensation Division 1510 E. Pershing Boulevard, Cheyenne, Wyoming 82002-0700; (307) 777-7441; Fax: (307) 777-6552.

Employers who employ workers in required (or extra-hazardous) industries or occupations as described within the state's workers compensation act—such as mining, heavy construction, lumber products, chemical products—must provide coverage for their employees through the state fund. This coverage for such employees is compulsory and may not be provided through a private carrier. Coverage for all other industries and occupations is optional at the choice of the employer and is not compulsory, either through the state fund or through a private carrier. Effective July 1, 1992, specific industries are excluded from coverage through the state fund unless coverage is elected for all employees. The elective coverage is in effect for a minimum three year period. Coverage may be withdrawn by the employer after the three year period if the employer is current on all contributions and payments required by the act.

Employer premiums are set through an industry based rating system with experience modification assigned after an employer has been registered in the state fund for two fiscal years.

Any nonresident employee and his nonresident employer who are temporarily engaged in work within the state of Wyoming are exempt from the provisions of Wyoming's workers compensation act. Wyoming residents employed by a nonresident employer in a required industry or occupation must be provided coverage through the Wyoming workers compensation act. Wyoming employers and employees covered under the state's workers compensation act but temporarily working out of state are still covered by the Wyoming law. Employers who hire workers in another state to perform work in the other state must provide coverage for those employees under the laws of the other state.

Nonresident employers who hire Wyoming resident employees in a required industry or occupation must complete and file an application for coverage with the Wyoming workers compensation division. A nonresident employer is defined as one who has not been domiciled in Wyoming for at least one year prior to commencing operations in the state.

The workers compensation act requires a minimum $10,000 surety bond for all nonresident employers required to register and provide coverage with the state fund. Employers performing work in Wyoming under contract are subject only to the $10,000 bond requirement if the contract amount does not exceed $100,000. For each additional $100,000 or fraction thereof of contract, an additional $1,000 is required, up to a maximum bond required of $50,000.

## Residual Markets

Workers compensation coverage is provided by private insurance companies in all but the five monopolistic states. Since workers compensation is a required coverage, it must be available to all businesses subject to the law. There are times, however, when businesses are unable to obtain insurance in the non-monopolistic states from insurance companies because of their size, the type of work they do, or poor workers compensation loss experience.

In response to this need, jurisdictions have established residual market systems, which sometimes are called the markets of last resort. There are two basic methods of providing insurance for the residual market.

Some states have established competitive state workers compensation funds. These funds compete with private insurers for desirable business in addition to providing insurance for companies that cannot obtain it in the open market. The state funds usually provide coverage only for operations within their states. Some of them are operated as independent insurance companies; some maintain their governmental agency structure.

An assigned risk system handles the residual market in another way. States that use this system assign residual business to private insurance companies who operate in the state. The assignments usually are based on the amount of business the insurer writes voluntarily in the state. Some insurers participate in the assigned risk system as reinsurers; others participate by directly providing coverage to those businesses assigned to them. Surcharges or premium differentials may apply to insureds who participate in an assigned risk program.

The state of Florida has established a joint underwriting association to handle the residual market there.

# Chapter 8

# Federal Workers Compensation Coverage

## Introduction

The United States Longshore and Harbor Workers Compensation Act (L&HWCA), 33 USC 901-952, was enacted in 1927, sixteen years after the first state workers compensation law was passed. The federal act was designed to provide the benefit of workers compensation to employees (other than seamen) who work in maritime employment upon the navigable waters of the United States and who are usually considered outside the scope of state compensation laws. Even so, the purpose of this federal compensation law is no different than that of a state compensation law; namely, to compensate workers for injuries that affect their wage earning capabilities and that arise out of the workers' employment.

The Jones Act, 46 USC 688, is a federal statute, the Merchant Marine Act of 1920, states that a seaman injured in the course of his employment by the negligence of the owner, master, or fellow crew member can recover damages for his injuries. The act states that any seaman who suffers injury in the course of his employment may maintain an action for damages directly against the owners of the ship, and in the case of death, the seaman's personal representative can maintain an action for wrongful death. Jurisdiction in such actions is under the court of the district in which the defendant employer resides or in which the principal office is located.

In addition to these federal laws, and as a way to comply with those laws while providing workers compensation insurance and employers liability insurance for affected workers, several endorsements are available for use.

47

This article offers a discussion of the L&HWCA, the Jones Act, and federal workers compensation endorsements. The endorsements are presented numerically.

## The Longshore and Harbor Workers Compensation Act

### Scope of Coverage

The coverage of the L&HWCA applies to compensation for disability or death of an employee if the disability or death results from injury occurring upon the navigable waters of the United States, including any adjoining pier, wharf, dry dock, terminal, marine railway, or other adjoining area customarily used in the loading, unloading, repairing, dismantling, or building of a vessel.

One of the original problems that arose with the L&HWCA was that anyone performing work however remotely connected to maritime employment attempted to obtain the benefits of the act. Therefore, in order to curb the jurisdictional scope of the act, not only does the coverage paragraph of the L&HWCA contain certain exclusions, but the definition of "employee" is limited to specific classes of workers.

The L&HWCA does not apply to an officer or employee of the U.S. government, any state or foreign government, or any city or county government; it also does not apply to an employee who is injured solely due to his own intoxication or due to his or a fellow employee's willful intention. The term "employee" means any person engaged in maritime employment, but this term *does not include* clerical, secretarial, security, or data processing work; it does not include individuals employed by a camp, restaurant, recreational operation, or retail outlet; nor does it include individuals employed by a marina, aquaculture workers, individuals employed to build, repair, or dismantle any recreational vessel under sixty-five feet in length. Masters or members of a crew of any vessel or any person engaged to load or unload or repair any small vessel under eighteen tons net are also not considered employees under the longshore act.

Needless to say, disputes and legal challenges over the definition of "employee" continue. The current judicial mood seems to be to decide each case on its own circumstances. An example of this thinking is in *Bienvenu v. Texaco, Inc.,* 164 F.3d 901 (5th Cir. 1999).

In this case, the United States Court of Appeals for the Fifth Circuit put forth an informative discussion of the history of the L&HWCA and judicial interpretation of its scope, but ended up showing that the trigger of coverage is decided on a case-by-case basis. Here, the injured worker, Bienvenu, was responsible for maintaining and calibrating automated equipment located on fixed production platforms. Bienvenu was injured while on board a boat that transported him around the various platforms and he claimed benefits under the L&HWCA. Benefits were denied on the grounds that Bienvenu was not engaged in maritime employment and spent the vast majority of his working hours on fixed platforms; indeed, the fact was that Bienvenu spent only one hour out of twelve actually performing work on navigable waters. Nevertheless, the appeals court ruled that Bienvenu was entitled to L&HWCA benefits and that the percentage of work time spent on navigable waters was substantial enough to trigger L&HWCA coverage.

Now, if courts continue to decide the scope of coverage under the L&HWCA on a case-by-case basis, employers and employees should know that judicial interpretations of the law may very well favor an emphasis on upholding the purpose of the law (to compensate workers for work related injuries) in contrast to a strict reading of the words and phrases of the act. Examples of this happening are: *Levins v. Benefits Review Board*, 724 F.2d 4 (1st Cir. 1984); *Parrott v. Seattle Joint Port Labor Relations Committee of the Pacific Maritime Ass'n and Insurance Co. of North America,* 22 BRBS 434 (1989); and *Bundens v. J.E. Brenneman Co.*, 46 F.3d 292 (3d Cir. 1995).

In the *Levins* case, a federal court stated that: "it is the employee's actual duties rather than a formal job classification that must be looked at in determining coverage." This was a case where a book clerk worked in the office, but also was required to work as a runner on the pier whenever ships under 300 tons were loaded or unloaded. The clerk was injured while working outside the office—he fell in a parking lot—and he sought benefits under the L&HWCA. The federal circuit court agreed with the clerk that he was a covered employee. In the *Parrott* case, an administrative law judge decided that a claimant's duties as a night dispatcher delivering slips to foremen aboard vessels constituted maritime employment within the coverage of the L&HWCA. And, in the *Bundens* case, it was decided that a construction worker building a dock was a harbor worker and covered by the Longshore Act.

## Employer's Liability

Section 904 of the Longshore Compensation Act states that every employer is liable for and shall secure the payment to his employees of the compensation payable under the requirements of the act. In the case of an employer who is a subcontractor, the contractor shall be liable for and shall secure the payment of such compensation to employees of the subcontractor unless the subcontractor has secured such payment.

This liability of the employer is exclusive and precludes all other liability of the employer to the employee, his legal representative, or his dependents. In other words, the exclusive remedy theory as applied to the employer. Of course, if the employer fails to secure payment of compensation, an injured employee can file suit at law or in admiralty for damages and the employer cannot use the defenses that were common prior to the enactment of workers compensation laws: negligence of a fellow servant; the assumption of risk by the employee; or contributory negligence on the part of the employee. Furthermore, if a responsible employer fails to secure the compensation required under the L&HWCA, he can be fined up to $10,000 or be sentenced to not more than one year imprisonment. This same punishment is meted out if the employer attempts to avoid the payment of compensation by transferring, selling, or concealing any property belonging to the employer.

So, any employer that does not fulfill his obligations under the L&HWCA faces not only the clear probability of a lawsuit filed by the injured employee, but also a statutory punishment.

## Third Party Actions

Having a party other than the employer involved in the injury of an employee is not a unique occurrence. The L&HWCA takes that into account whether the injury is caused by a person or a vessel. In the event of injury to an employee covered under the L&HWCA caused by the negligence of a vessel, the employee can bring an action against that vessel (an in rem action alleging negligence against the vessel owner) as a third party. Should that happen, the employer is not liable to the vessel for such damages directly or indirectly and any agreements or warranties to the contrary shall be void. Therefore, hold harmless agreements and third-party-over actions are precluded by the L&HWCA.

It should be noted that the third party liability of vessels is the subject of section 905 (b) of the L&HWCA. Section 933 of the act applies to compensation for injuries in which third persons are liable. An injured employee can file suit or a claim against a third person who is liable for the injuries. However, should the employee accept compensation from the employer under an award in an order filed by an administrative law judge, that operates as an assignment to the employer of all rights of the employee to recover damages against the third person. The employer then has ninety days after the assignment to bring an action against the third person; if he fails to do so, the right reverts to the employee.

## Compensation

The L&HWCA lists levels of compensation for disability or death under various sections. For example, the maximum rate of compensation of weekly benefits cannot exceed an amount equal to 200 percent of the applicable national average weekly wage as determined by the Secretary of Labor. Also, compensation for loss of hearing in one ear is fifty-two weeks pay; for loss of hearing in both ears, 200 weeks. The "proper and equitable" compensation for serious disfigurement of the face, neck, or head cannot exceed $7,500. Reasonable funeral expenses are not to exceed $3,000. Of course, these amounts can be revised either by law or by increases caused by inflation.

## The L&HWCA and the Workers Compensation Policy

Longshore and Harbor Workers Compensation Act insurance may be provided by attaching endorsement WC 00 01 06 A to the standard workers compensation and employers liability insurance policy. The endorsement applies to work done in the states scheduled (including those states with a monopolistic state fund) and extends the definition of workers compensation law to include the L&HWCA; this is necessary because the policy declares in the general section that the term "workers compensation law" does not include any federal workers compensation law. The statutory obligation of an employer to furnish benefits required by the L&HWCA is thus satisfied. The coverage, exclusions, and conditions of part one of the workers compensation policy are applied to those parties involved under the L&HWCA.

Under part two of the workers compensation policy—employers liability insurance—the insurance applies to bodily injury by accident or by disease arising out of and in the course of the injured employee's employment. However, exclusion 8 precludes employers liability insurance from bodily injury to any person in work subject to the L&HWCA; endorsement WC 00 01 06 A drops this exclusion as it relates to such work. For operations subject to the L&HWCA, the standard limits of liability under part two of the policy are: $100,000 per each accident for bodily injury by accident; $100,000 per each employee for bodily injury by disease; and a $500,000 policy limit for bodily injury by disease. Increased limits are, of course, available for an additional premium.

The coverage, most of the exclusions, and conditions of the employers liability insurance are applicable to those parties covered by the L&HWCA. Now, since such insurance pays for damages for which the insured may become liable to a third party based on a third-party-over action, a question may arise. The L&HWCA precludes third-party-over actions, but the insurance policy of the insured has an insuring agreement that states that any liability damages based on such actions will be paid. Is there a contradiction present? No, because the insuring agreement on the workers compensation policy declares that the damages will be paid *where recovery is permitted by law*. Since the law (the L&HWCA) does not permit third-party-over actions against the employer (the insured), the issue is moot.

## State vs. Federal Coverage

Based on the nature of the work involved, with accidents and injuries happening on land as well as on or over water, conflicts may arise over which coverage takes precedence: state or federal. For example, in *Logan v. Louisiana Dock Co.*, 541 So.2d 182 (La. 1989), Logan, the employee, was injured while repairing a barge on the defendant's dry dock. He filed for workers compensation and sued to obtain benefits. Louisiana Dry Dock responded that Logan could have sought benefits under the L&HWCA and so, he was not eligible for state workers compensation. A Louisiana court of appeals decided that just because there is a federal remedy, that does not necessarily mean there is no state remedy. The court, in finding for Logan, held that the L&HWCA does not expressly say that it is the exclusive remedy for injured workers; the proper approach is for state workers compensation laws to complement the federal law.

This feeling represents the current judicial attitude. Indeed, the U.S. Supreme Court has decreed that state workers compensation laws and the L&HWCA are not mutually exclusive remedies and has, in effect, sanctioned the filing of a claim by longshoremen under both the federal law and the state law. In *Sun Ship, Inc. v. Pennsylvania*, 447 U.S. 715 (1980), and in *Herb's Welding, Inc. v. Gray*, 470 U.S. 414 (1985), the Supreme Court held that the L&HWCA supplements rather than replaces the state workers compensation law and that concurrent jurisdiction exists for land based maritime injuries.

It should be noted that recent amendments to the L&HWCA do require that a worker or dependent who is excluded from the definition of "employee" must first claim compensation under the appropriate state workers compensation program and receive a final decision on the merits of that claim before any claim may be filed under the Longshore and Harbor Workers Compensation Act.

# The Jones Act

## Scope of Coverage

Seamen are subject to admiralty law and, if injured, have the right to file claims for damages in admiralty courts where the proceeding is in the nature of a liability suit against the employer based on negligence. The Jones Act allows for the providing of insurance for such liability through the use of the standard workers compensation and employers liability policy and endorsements. There are two programs available to furnish such insurance.

Under program I, the workers compensation policy has endorsement WC 00 02 01 A, the maritime coverage endorsement, attached to it. This endorsement does not address the workers compensation insurance part of the workers compensation policy. Furthermore, the workers compensation law definition does not include any federal workers compensation law. So, endorsement WC 00 02 01 A is not relevant to the workers compensation insurance part of the workers compensation policy. WC 00 02 01 A does state that the insurance afforded by the employers liability insurance part of the workers compensation policy for bodily injury to a master or member of the crew of a vessel is changed by the provisions of the endorsement. The endorsement applies the insurance to bodily injury by accident or by disease arising out of and in the course of the injured employee's employment that is described in the schedule on WC 00 02 01 A. The bodily injury must occur in the territorial limits of, or in the operation of a vessel sailing directly between the ports of, the United States of America or Canada. And, note that the injured worker must sue for damages under the Jones Act. This is in keeping with the nature of employers liability insurance since that coverage is based on sums that the insured "legally must pay as damages."

The employers liability insurance part of the workers compensation policy has several exclusions, and, for the most part, these exclusions do apply to any claims made by seamen against the insured. The endorsement deletes exclusion 10 pertaining to bodily injury to a master or member of the crew of any vessel. And, endorsement WC 00 02 01 A adds two other exclusions. These two exclusions deal with items that are peculiar to maritime coverage insurance.

The first exclusion applies to bodily injury covered by a protection and indemnity (P&I) policy issued to the named insured. P&I coverage is an ocean marine form that provides legal liability coverage for marine exposures. For example, if a third party is injured in a collision with the insured's vessel, the

P&I policy will respond to a claim. The exclusion on endorsement WC 00 02 01 A aims to prevent any injured party from an attempt to stack coverages since the endorsement does apply to bodily injury by accident.

The second exclusion states that the insurance does not cover the named insured's duty to provide transportation, wages, maintenance, and care. These items are considered historical rights given to sailors and one of the elements of the contract of hire. A sailor who falls sick in the service of the vessel has historically been entitled to wages, transportation back home, food and quarters to the end of the voyage, medical attention, and other similar services. The exclusion on WC 00 02 01 A makes the point that the insurer does not substitute itself for the insured in fulfilling an ancient common law of the sea. However, it needs to be noted that the insurer will drop this exclusion if the insured wants the coverage and will pay an additional premium.

Endorsement WC 00 02 01 A does limit the damages paid for bodily injury by accident and by disease; bodily injury by accident is on an each accident basis, and injury by disease is on an aggregate basis. Both items have the limits of liability scheduled on the endorsement and the insurer states clearly that it will not pay any claims after the applicable limits have been reached.

Under program II, the same coverage in program I is offered, along with the addition of voluntary compensation. The insurer agrees under this program to offer a settlement of a claim voluntarily in accordance with the statutory benefits called for by the workers compensation law of the state(s) specified on the voluntary compensation endorsement, WC 00 02 03. If the offer of a settlement is rejected, employers liability then will apply to such a claim or suit. Endorsement WC 00 02 03 applies insurance to bodily injury by accident or by disease sustained by an employee who is a master or member of the crew of a vessel described in the schedule. The bodily injury must occur in employment that is necessary or incidental to work scheduled on the endorsement.

The insurance provided by the endorsement does not cover any obligation imposed by a workers compensation law or bodily injury intentionally caused by the named insured. Furthermore, before any benefits are paid, the persons entitled to them must sign a release, transfer to the insurer all rights of recovery, and cooperate with the insurer in enforcing the right to recover from others. If the persons entitled to the benefits fail to do these things, then the duty of the insurer to pay ends at once.

## Definition of "Seaman"

Since the Jones Act deals with the recovery for injury to or death of a *seaman*, that term needs to be examined. Lacking a concrete definition in the act itself, courts have established through judicial decisions certain factors that need to be met if a claimant is considered a seaman. Some of these factors are: the vessel on which the claimant is employed must be in navigable waters; the claimant must have a more or less permanent connection with the vessel, like performing a substantial part of his work on the vessel; and the claimant must be aboard to aid in the navigation of the vessel, as in the actual operation or maintenance of the vessel.

The U.S. Supreme Court attempted to clarify this somewhat in a 1995 case. In *Chandris, Inc. v. Latsis*, 515 U.S. 347 (1995), the Supreme Court said that a seaman must contribute to the function of the vessel and that his or her connection to a vessel must be substantial in both duration and nature. And, the Court added that as a rule of thumb, a seaman should spend more than 30 percent of his or her time on the vessel. Since that time, lower courts have tried to use this direction from the Supreme Court to determine just what a seaman is, on a case-by-case basis. In 1997, the Supreme Court took another shot at clarifying the issue. The case is *Harbor Tug & Barge Co. v. Papai*, 520 U.S. 548 (1997).

In that case, a worker was injured while on a one day assignment obtained through the union hiring hall to paint a tug at dockside. This worker fell from a ladder and hurt his leg. He sued for benefits under the Jones Act and, after the trial court decided he was not a seaman and could not receive Jones Act benefits, an appeals court declared that he was a seaman. The Supreme Court took the case and agreed with the trial court. The Court said that defining a seaman under the Jones Act is a mixed question of law and fact, but that coverage under the act should be confined to those who face a regular exposure to the perils of the sea; land based employment is inconsistent with the Jones Act.

The Court reaffirmed its ruling in the *Chandris* case and sought to further clarify that ruling. Essential requirements for a person to be a seaman are: there must be a substantial connection between the employee and the vessel in navigation, substantial in terms of both duration and nature; and, the employee's duties must contribute to the function of the vessel or to the accomplishment of the vessel's mission. The Court went on to declare that the fundamental purpose of the "substantial connection" requirement is to give full effect to the remedial scheme created by Congress, that is, to separate sea based maritime workers from land based workers who are not regularly exposed to the perils of the sea. These latter workers can seek benefits under the Longshore and Harbor Workers Compensation Act.

## Jurisdiction of the Jones Act

The Jones Act provides that jurisdiction over actions for personal injuries is in a court of the district where the defendant employer resides or where the principal office is located. The maritime coverage endorsement (WC 00 02 01 A) states that if the insured is sued, the original suit must be brought in the U.S. or Canada. Based on these phrases, a question may arise: should an injured seaman file a lawsuit based on the Jones Act in a state court or a federal court? The Jones Act is, after all, a federal law; at the same time, insurance coverage under the Jones Act can be provided by a policy used to comply with state workers compensation requirements.

Court decisions through the years have supported the proposition that federal and state courts have concurrent jurisdiction to enforce the right of action established by the Jones Act. However, since the act is a federal law, federal principles of law and rules of construction prevail if a conflict arises with a state law. For example, if an injured seaman files an action under the Jones Act in a state court, that court must use federal rules on the introduction and use of evidence regardless of the state regulations that exist. So a seaman has his choice of courts should he feel the need to file a lawsuit against his employer.

Concurrent jurisdiction is accepted, but what about dual recovery? Can an injured seaman accept recovery under both the Jones Act and a state workers compensation law? In perhaps a trend-setting case in Louisiana, a federal court decided that a workers compensation action is not precluded under the Jones Act under certain circumstances. The court, in *Dominick v. Houtech Inland Well Service, Inc.*, 718 F.Supp. 489 (E.D.La. 1989), indicated that since the state supreme court had ruled that insurance carried by the employer was considered insurance for state workers compensation purposes regardless of the fact that it may have been purchased by the employer as insurance for Jones Act claims, a workers compensation claim was maintainable. Thus, the injured seaman had two avenues for recovery for his claim open to him.

There are two points to remember, however, on this subject. First, the Jones Act as a federal law has precedence over conflicting state laws if indeed there is conflict. For example, if the Jones Act allowed compensation to injured seamen and a state law forbad such compensation, the Jones Act would supersede the state law. However, in areas where the state law does not conflict with the Jones Act, both laws can peacefully coexist. So, where a state allows a workers compensation action for pain and suffering incurred prior to death or allows action against tortfeasors other than employers, seamen that are injured in that state receive the benefit of the state laws. The state laws complement the federal law and an injured worker receives his just compensation.

The second point is that, historically, courts have allowed offsets for concurrent awards. So if a seaman receives compensation under the Jones Act for his injury, and then files a state workers compensation claim based on that same injury, a court may allow the workers compensation action as permitted by state law, but will offset any award by the amount already received. Thus, the possibility of double recovery being an unlimited source of compensation is remote.

## Federal Workers Compensation Endorsements

There are some federal laws pertaining to workers compensation that affect workers employed in areas that are beyond the authority of an individual state. As a way to comply with these laws, several endorsements are available for use with the workers compensation policy.

### Defense Base Act Coverage Endorsement WC 00 01 01 A

This endorsement applies only to the work described in the schedule or described on the information page as subject to the Defense Base Act. Basically, WC 00 01 01 A modifies the workers compensation and employers liability insurance policy by replacing the definition of "workers compensation law" found on the policy with the following meaning: workers compensation law means the workers compensation law and occupational disease law of each state or territory named in Item 3.A. of the information page *and* the Defense Base Act (42 USC Sections 1651-1654). The definition goes on to state that it does not include any other federal workers compensation law or federal occupational disease law. As an example of putting WC 00 01 01 A to work, it can be used for contractors performing work at overseas military bases or under various public works contracts outside the continental United States of America.

This endorsement also declares that exclusion 8 under the employers liability insurance part of the workers compensation policy does not apply to work subject to the Defense Base Act. Exclusion 8 deals with bodily injury to any person in work subject to the Defense Base Act.

WC 00 01 01 A applies the workers compensation policy to the described work as though the location included in the description of the work were a state named on the workers compensation information page; therefore, the description of the work *must* include the location where the work is to be performed.

## Federal Coal Mine Health and Safety Act
## Coverage Endorsement WC 00 01 02

This endorsement is used when the workers compensation policy is to cover exposures subject to the Federal Coal Mine Health and Safety Act. WC 00 01 02 states that the definition of workers compensation law includes the Coal Mine Act and applies only to work in a state shown in the schedule.

Workers compensation insurance applies under this endorsement to bodily injury by disease that is caused or aggravated by the conditions of the employment and the employee's last day of exposure to the conditions causing or aggravating such bodily injury by disease must occur during the policy period.

## Federal Employers Liability Act
## Coverage Endorsement WC 00 01 04

This endorsement applies only to work subject to the Federal Employers Liability Act (45 USC sections 51 - 60) and any amendment to that act in effect during the policy period. For example, the act makes an interstate railroad liable for bodily injuries sustained by an employee if the injured employee can show any negligence on the part of the railroad. Due to the interstate nature of the employment, such employees are not subject to state workers compensation laws and this endorsement covers the liability of the railroad.

The liability to pay for damages is limited and the limits are shown in the schedule. The limits of liability for bodily injury by accident are on an each accident basis; the limits for bodily injury by disease are on an aggregate basis.

## Longshore and Harbor Workers Compensation Act
## Coverage Endorsement WC 00 01 06 A

This endorsement applies only to work subject to the Longshore and Harbor Workers Compensation Act in a state shown in the schedule and provides compensation coverage to employees such as longshoremen, harbor workers, ship repairmen, and shipbuilders. The endorsement is attached to the workers compensation and employers liability insurance policy (WC 00 00

00) and expands the definition of workers compensation law to include the Longshore and Harbor Workers Compensation Act (33 USC sections 901 - 950) and any amendments to that act that are in effect during the policy period.

WC 00 01 06 A declares that exclusion 8 under the employers liability insurance part of the workers compensation policy does not apply to work subject to the Longshore and Harbor Workers Compensation Act. This is, of course, similar to the wording found on endorsement WC 00 01 01 A as noted above. It is also stated on the Longshore and Harbor Workers Compensation Act coverage endorsement that the endorsement does not apply to the Defense Base Act, the Outer Continental Shelf Lands Act, or the Nonappropriated Fund Instrumentalities Act.

## Nonappropriated Fund Instrumentalities Act
## Coverage Endorsement WC 00 01 08 A

This endorsement applies only to the work described in the schedule as subject to the Nonappropriated Fund Instrumentalities Act; the definition of "workers compensation law" is expanded by this endorsement to include the Nonappropriated Fund Instrumentalities Act. This act makes the Longshore and Harbor Workers Compensation Act apply to civilian employees of certain entities, such as, the army exchange service or the military motion picture service. Thus, workers compensation insurance and employers liability insurance is provided for those civilian companies and employees that administer the stores or dining areas that exist on military bases.

WC 00 01 08 A also notes that exclusion 8 of the employers liability insurance part of the workers compensation policy does not apply to work subject to the Instrumentalities Act.

## Outer Continental Shelf Lands Act
## Coverage Endorsement WC 00 01 09 A

This endorsement applies only to the work described in the schedule as subject to the Outer Continental Shelf Lands Act. The coverage will apply to that work as though the location shown in the schedule were a state named on the workers compensation policy. Therefore, the description of the work must show the state whose boundaries, if extended to the outer continental shelf, would include the location of the work. The Outer Continental Shelf Lands Act makes the Longshore and Harbor Workers Compensation Act apply to work involving the development of the natural resources of the outer continental shelf. Workers who are employed in this type of activity receive workers compensation insurance, and employers of such workers receive employers liability insurance through this particular endorsement.

WC 00 01 09 A, like the previous endorsements noted above, expands the meaning of "workers compensation law" to include the particular law for which this endorsement is named and deletes exclusion 8 from the employers liability insurance part of the workers compensation policy.

## Maritime Coverage Endorsement WC 00 02 01 A

Masters and members of the crews of vessels are not covered under state workers compensation laws or under the Longshore and Harbor Workers Compensation Act. They are subject to admiralty law and, if injured, have the right to sue their employers for damages. This endorsement affords coverage where the employer has such exposure and needs employers liability insurance.

This endorsement applies to and schedules limits of liability for bodily injury by accident or by disease. Such bodily injury must arise out of and in the course of employment as described in the schedule. The coverage does not apply to bodily injury that is covered by a protection and indemnity policy issued to the insured (a protection and indemnity policy is ocean marine insurance that applies to personal injury liability including bodily injury to employees). Insurance under this endorsement also does not apply to the duty of the insured to provide transportation, wages, maintenance, and cure for the employees unless the insured pays an extra premium for such coverage and this is noted in the schedule.

WC 00 02 01 A goes on to state that exclusion 10 under the employers liability insurance part of the workers compensation policy is removed; exclusion 10 deals with bodily injury to a master or member of the crew of any vessel.

In the early history of ocean marine insurance, an injured seaman could file an action in rem to seek compensation for his injury. In such an action, the seaman filed a suit directly against the ship and not the owner, thereby seeking compensation by claiming a property interest in the ship and bypassing the problem of whether or not the ship owner carried liability insurance. An endorsement did exist that provided coverage for such in rem lawsuits, but that endorsement is now obsolete since WC 00 02 01 A includes a statement that a suit or action in rem against a vessel owned by the insured is treated by the insurer as a suit against the insured himself requiring a defense by the insurance company.

# Chapter 9

# Premium

Part five of the workers compensation and employers liability policy deals with premium. This chapter offers a review of that part of the policy and a practical lesson in the ways in which a typical policy premium is reached. This latter item highlights areas such as risk classifications, discounts, and loss/expense constants.

## Manuals

The first clause in the premium section of the workers compensation policy notes that all premium for the policy is determined by the insurer's manuals of rules, rates, rating plans, and classifications. The insurer claims the role as guide for determining premiums that will be paid by the insured. The insured can affect the premium by risk management efforts, loss history, deductibles, and other methods; but it is the insurer that ultimately determines the premium charged for the workers compensation/employers liability exposures presented by the insured.

## Classifications

Classifications are categories into which the insurer puts the insured to properly gauge the risks of workers compensation losses that the insured will face over the policy period. The classification is based on information supplied mainly by the insured. This clause tells the insured how the insurer views, or classifies, the business of the insured, and how that classification leads to the premium charge.

A reference is made in this clause to Item 4 of the information page, reminding the insured that Item 4 shows the rate and premium basis for the work classifications that were assigned by the insurer to the insured. The classifications were made based on the information supplied by the insured to the insurer, and that information is subject to verification and change by audit.

## Remuneration

This clause tells the insured what the basis is for the premium charge. The premium is determined by multiplying a rate times a premium basis, which is *remuneration*. This term includes payroll and all other remuneration paid or payable during the policy period for the services of all the officers and employees engaged in the work of the insured that is covered by the workers compensation policy and all other persons engaged in work that could make the insurer liable under the workers compensation insurance part of the policy. The rate is charged per $100 of remuneration.

The exposure for workers who are not on the insured's regular payroll, but who still represent a risk for workers compensation, is handled through the use of the contract price between the insured and these workers as a premium basis. If these workers have workers compensation coverage through other employers, the risk of loss is lessened for the insured and the insurer, and so, there is no need to charge for that exposure. The insured employer must give the insurer proof that the employers of these particular workers have lawfully secured workers compensation obligations. The method of proof is not spelled out in the clause, but insurers will certainly let the insured know exactly what is needed.

## Premium Payments

The premium payments clause notes that the employer named in Item 1 of the information page is required to pay all premium when due. In the event of multiple named insureds, the first named insured has the responsibility for the payment. This latter phrase is not in this particular clause, but, under the conditions section of the policy, the first named insured is tapped as the representative of all insureds. So, that entity has the duty to make the premium payments to the insurer.

## Final Premium

The premium shown on the information page is an estimate. The final premium is determined after the policy ends by using the actual, not the estimated, premium basis and the proper classifications and rates that lawfully apply to the work covered by the policy. Since the premium basis (remuneration) may change during the policy period, an adequate premium charge is more properly figured at the end of the policy period when the true extent of the exposures is known by the insurer. If the final premium is more than the estimated premium paid by the insured, the difference must be paid to the insurer. If the situation is reversed, a refund will be made by the insurer to the first named insured.

The insured is informed here that the policy has a minimum premium, that is, a charge that will be paid regardless of the actual remuneration. This minimum premium is the highest minimum premium for the classifications covered by the policy. This charge is made to cover the expenses that the insurer has incurred in underwriting and issuing the workers compensation policy.

This clause also determines the amount of premium in case the policy is cancelled. If the insurer cancels the policy, the final premium is calculated on a pro rata basis, based on the time the policy was in force. If the insured cancels the policy, the final premium is based on the time the policy was in force plus the short-rate cancellation table and procedures of the insurer. Note that a final premium figured on the basis of an insured-cancelled policy will be more than one figured on an insurer-cancelled basis.

The rating manual makes an exception for the short-rate cancellation penalty. It does not apply if the insured retires from all business covered by the policy, sells the business, or completes all work covered by the policy.

## Records

The insurer needs information about the risk to charge a proper premium, and the insured is required to help in this endeavor. This clause requires the insured not only to keep records, but also to provide copies of them to the insurer when asked.

## Audit

The insurer is given the right to examine and audit all the records of the insured that relate to the policy. Such records include ledgers, journals, registers, vouchers, contracts, tax reports, payroll and disbursement records, and programs for storing and retrieving data. The insurer needs such information to properly understand the business of the insured and the workers compensation risks that face the insured and to set the needed premium to adequately cover those risks.

The insurer may conduct audits during regular business hours during the policy period and within three years after the policy period ends. The information developed by the audits is used to determine the final premium.

# Practical Information

## Workers Compensation Bureaus

The workers compensation and employers liability insurance policy is a contract that binds the insurance company to the insured for worker injuries. In general the policy offers protection for exposures that are delineated by the workers compensation laws of the states in which the insured company has business operations.

Most states require that workers compensation and employers liability policy forms be filed with their insurance departments for approval. The National Council on Compensation Insurance, Inc. (NCCI) files forms on behalf of its member states. In other states, independent bureaus file forms for their members. There also are five monopolistic states, in which workers compensation insurance may be written by the state insurance fund. Additional information on monopolistic state funds is available in Chapter 7.

In addition to issuing forms, the NCCI and other independent bureaus establish the rules for classification and premium determination. Experience rating, retrospective rating, and other rating information also are developed by these rating bureaus. Information in this section is based primarily on NCCI rules, but there may be variations by state.

## Classification of Exposures

In general, the idea of classifying workers is to group employers by the type of work they do. The business of the employer is classified, not the individual types of operations within the business. This is called the *governing classification*. After the one governing basic classification is assigned, secondary classifications may be assigned when:

- The basic classification requires that certain operations or employees be separately rated.
- The insured may engage in construction or erection, farm, repair, or mercantile operations that require additional basic classifications.
- The insured operates more than one business in a state.

All employees are assigned to the principal business classification if its rate is the same or higher than that of the secondary business classification that applies to the employees. However, the secondary business classification is used if it is higher.

The NCCI rules state that in addition to the basic business classification, there are standard exception and general exclusion operations that are classified separately. The standard exception classifications are clerical office; clerical or drafting telecommuter; drafting; drivers, chauffeurs, and their helpers; and outside salespersons, collectors, or messengers.

General exclusions are aircraft operations, new construction or alterations, stevedoring, sawmill operations, and employer-operated daycare services. These types of work are classified separately unless specifically included in the basic classification wording.

For example, a retail supermarket is classified as a supermarket at, perhaps, a rate of $5.00 or more per $100 of payroll. This is the basic business classification. A clerical office rate—which is a standard exception classification—in this company's state of domicile is less than $.50 per $100 of payroll. Because of this, the supermarket owner may try to classify managers and service desk workers as clerical rather than supermarket employees. The reasoning is that the managers do not physically work in the supermarket operation; they do clerical tasks and manage the operation.

However, in order to qualify for the lower rated clerical office classification, the clerical work area must be *separated and distinguishable* from all other areas and hazards of the supermarket by *floors, walls, partitions, counters, or other physical barriers.* Based on this description, managers who spend part of their time in a partitioned office but also walk through the store even on rare occasions cannot be classified as clerical. Their payroll must be included in the supermarket payroll. The reason for this is that such individuals are subject to the same exposures (armed robbery, slipping and falling on loose produce, items falling from shelves, etc.) as a cashier or stocking clerk.

There may be disagreement between the insured and insurer over whether service desk workers in a retail operation, who spend their time behind a glass partition, may be classified as clerical. They probably cannot be included as clerical because, after all, they are subject to the main exposures of the store and not removed from the general retail area.

Some employees may do more than one type of work. In this case the NCCI rules permit the employees' payroll to be divided among different classifications as long as the employer maintains payroll records by classification for each individual.

When classification disputes between an insured and insurer arise, either may request a classification audit by the applicable rating bureau. Once such an audit is completed, it becomes more difficult to reassign payroll to a different classification.

## Premium Basis

The premium basis for the vast majority of classifications is remuneration. A few classifications do not use payroll. For example, domestic workers may be classified on a per capita basis when using NCCI rules. Remuneration includes money or substitutes for money, such as the value of lodging or meals as part of pay. Most states include the regular pay portion of overtime pay, bonuses, and items such as store merchandise as remuneration. Specific state rules should be consulted for unusual situations regarding remuneration. The key to assigning payroll lies in keeping accurate and valid payroll records by class.

## Payroll Limitation

Most states include an insured's executive officers under their workers compensation laws. In some states, executive officers may opt out of the system. When executive officers are included for coverage, their payroll is limited for reporting purposes. Each state sets minimum and maximum reporting thresholds. For example, the minimum payroll for an executive officer that must be reported to the workers compensation carrier may be $100 a week—even if he does not draw any salary. The maximum may be $1,000 a week, even though she actually is paid much more than $52,000 a year. A few classifications also limit the payroll that must be reported. Individual classifications should be reviewed to see if the payroll is limited.

Another aspect of payroll reporting that may cause confusion is wages for time not worked. For example, a company may require that employees work seven hours a day, five days a week. However, they are paid for eight hours a day. This is called a paid lunch hour. The entire amount of wages paid for this idle time must be reported to the carrier.

## Rates

There are two basic types of authorized rates used for workers compensation coverage. They are *manual rates* and rates developed by carriers that use *advisory loss costs or rates* as the basis. Individual states must approve the *authorized rate* that is used in their jurisdictions.

The authorized rate may be a manual rate. In states that authorize only manual rates, the rates are approved by the state insurance regulatory authority and must be used by each individual carrier as a starting point. The standard or manual premium for each insured is the same, regardless of which carrier quotes the coverage. However, variations in premium are developed when the insurance company applies credits or debits to the manual premium or applies filed deviations to the rates themselves. Carriers also may offer various back-end financial plans that serve to change the ultimate premium.

In other states, regulators approve individual advisory loss costs for each workers compensation classification. The advisory loss cost is the portion of the rate that represents expected losses per $100 of payroll for that class. Individual insurance companies then develop final rates by loading their expenses onto the advisory loss rates.

## Other Factors

Most states also authorize the use of an *expense constant*, which is a charge to cover expenses that are common to all workers compensation policies regardless of size. The amount of the expense constant varies by state, but it usually falls within the range of $100-200 per policy. If an insured's policy covers more than one state, only one expense constant is used—the highest from all the applicable states. There also is a *minimum premium* that is set on a state-by-state basis. It is the lowest premium required to provide coverage under a standard policy.

The next factor to be considered is called the *premium discount*. The relative expense of issuing and servicing a policy that has a large premium is lower than for policies that develop a smaller premium. The premium discount is a percentage credit that floats with the premium size. In other words, policies with higher premiums are given higher premium discounts than those with lower premiums. The applicable state rating bureaus issue tables that list the ascending premium discount percentages. There are different tables for stock and non-stock insurance companies.

There are a number of discount tables, depending upon the type of carrier and policy being issued. However, a range of premium discounts issued by the NCCI is as follows:

---

### Premium Discounts for Workers Compensation and Employers Liability Insurance
(Represent NCCI Tables 1-8)

| Standard Premium | Stock Carrier | Non-stock carrier |
| --- | --- | --- |
| First $5,000 | 0% | 0% |
| Next $95,000 | 9.5-10.9% | 2.0-3.5% |
| Next $400,000 | 11.9-12.6% | 4.0-5.0% |
| Over $500,000 | 12.4-14.4% | 6.0-7.0% |

Source: National Council on Compensation Insurance. Copyright 1995-1997. Information used with permission of the NCCI.

---

## Limits of Liability

As stated previously, there is no limit of liability in the standard workers compensation policy. The policy provides the statutory benefits that are required by the state in which the coverage applies. However, there is a limit of liability for part B of the policy, which is the employers liability section.

The standard employers liability limits are
Bodily injury by accident ......................... $100,000 each accident
Bodily injury by disease ........................... $500,000 policy limit
Bodily injury by disease ......................... $100,000 each employee

Some insureds need higher employers liability limits to satisfy the requirements of a commercial umbrella policy, a lender, or a party with whom they are contracting. Employer liability limits of up to $10,000,000 for each area of employers liability coverage are available. The additional premium charge ranges from 1.7 to 9 percent of the policy premium, depending on how much the employers liability limits are increased.

## Sample Premium Calculation

Following is a sample premium calculation. It illustrates how the various items that affect premium are shown on a policy. This is a fictitious insured, and the rates that are shown are for illustration purposes only.

# Extension of Information Page

## Item 4

| Classification | Code No. | Premium Basis Total Estimated Annual Remuneration | Rate Per $100 of Remuneration | Estimated Annual Premium |
|---|---|---|---|---|
| Salespersons - Outside | 8742 | $ 585,000 | 1.17 | $ 6,844 |
| Clerical Office Employees NOC | 8810 | 1,100,000 | .32 | $3,520 |
| Increased Limits Part Two | | | 1.9% | $   197 |
| Total Estimated Standard Premium | | | | $ 10,561 |
| Experience Modification | | | 1.05 | $   528 |
| Estimated Modified Premium | | | | $ 11,089 |
| Premium Discount | | | | -$   664 |
| Expense Constant | | | | $   200 |
| **Estimated Annual Premium** | | | | **$ 10,625** |

# Chapter 10

# Experience Rating

## Introduction

Experience rating compares a company's workers compensation losses with those of businesses engaged in similar types of work. The comparison results in an experience modification that may increase or decrease the company's workers compensation premium.

Experience rating is mandatory for all eligible insureds. Businesses may not cancel, rewrite, or extend a workers compensation policy in an attempt to avoid experience rating or qualify for or avoid a change in their experience modifications. Eligibility is determined by the amount of qualifying premium that an insured generates. States vary in their premium thresholds, but they range from $2,250 to $5,500 in average annual premium. Specific information on the qualifying premium is available from the NCCI or other applicable independent rating organizations.

The NCCI experience modification plan applies in forty-four jurisdictions (forty-three states and the District of Columbia). Independent experience rating plans apply in seven states: California, Delaware, Michigan, New Jersey, New York, Pennsylvania, and Texas. This discussion centers on the NCCI plan, which provides a framework for understanding experience rating. It is important, however, to check state regulations for differences.

## General Points

There are several general items to consider about experience rating:

- Loss data is used to adjust *future* premiums; that is, experience rating is prospective.

71

- Experience modifications generally are developed on an annual basis and are effective for a period of twelve months.
- Only one experience modification is applied to a risk at any one time. That experience modification applies to *all operations* of the risk. A risk is defined as all entities eligible for combination under the plan, regardless of whether one or more insurance policies are used to insure them.
- The expected losses used to develop experience modifications are based on the losses that are expected for all business in the insured's class. For example, the expected losses for a specific manufacturer would be compared with the expected losses for all manufacturers *as a class*.
- Schedule rating usually is permitted in addition to experience rating.
- Experience rating can substantially affect the amount of workers compensation premium that a business must pay. It provides a direct correlation between claims history and premium.

## The Mod

Under the NCCI plan, an experience modification factor, which often is referred to as the experience mod or mod, of less than 1.0 means that the firm will get a credit on its premium. A mod greater than 1.0 means that a debit will apply. A 1.0 mod is referred to as a *unity* modification.

For example, a mod of 1.25 indicates that the company will pay 25 percent more in premium than the average firm in its class because of its poor loss experience. A mod of .85 means that the company will get a 15 percent reduction from the standard rate because it has generated better-than-average loss experience.

Company A has an estimated standard premium of $25,000 and a mod of 1.25. It pays an additional $6,250 a year for workers compensation insurance because of poor loss experience. The 1.25 mod generates an annual premium for company A of $31,250. One of its direct competitors, Company B, has a modifier of .85. Company B, again with a standard premium of $25,000, pays only $21,250 for workers compensation coverage. Company B's premium is *$10,000 less* than what Company A has to pay. A business has to sell a lot of loaves of bread or widgets to make up $10,000 in bottom line costs to its competitor.

A mod is based on three years of the company's loss history. The most current year is omitted from the calculation. To illustrate, assume that a company purchases an experience-rated workers compensation policy with an inception date of January 10, 2001. Also assume that it purchased annual policies for the previous four years on January 10 of each year. The mod that is effective January 10, 2001, is based on the premium and losses for policy years January 10, 1999-2000; January 10, 1998-99; and January 10, 1997-98. Experience from the January 10, 2000-01, policy year does not enter the calculation the January 10, 2002, mod is calculated, at which time the 1997-98 year drops out of the calculation.

While three years of experience normally is used, up to three and three-fourths years of experience can be used in certain situations. There also are situations in which a newly organized business may apply for experience rating after being in business for only two years.

## Anniversary Rating Date

The normal *anniversary rating date* is the effective month and day when experience modification and rate changes take effect. The anniversary rating date usually corresponds to policy inception date. However, it may differ if prior policy years were longer or shorter than twelve months in duration. Experience mods usually are effective for twelve months and cannot be used longer than fifteen months.

An insured cannot cancel an existing workers compensation policy before its normal expiration date in order to take advantage of a decrease in compensation rates or experience modification. Even if the policy were canceled and rewritten midterm, the lower rates and experience modification would not apply to the new policy until the insured's normal anniversary rating date.

### Example #1
In this example, Meridian Manufacturers has an experience modification that is effective April 1, 2000. It applies to a policy with an effective date of April 1, 2000 or to any policy with an effective date up to July 1, 2000. If Meridian decides to change its policy renewal date from April 1 to July 1, so that it coincides with its fiscal year, the April 1 anniversary rating date is used for the entire fifteen months. At the end of the fifteen months (July 1, 2001), a new experience modification applies and the normal anniversary rating date changes to July 1.

In addition, rates that were in effect for the policy on April 1 will apply until July 1, 2000.

## Example #2

In this case, Meridian Manufacturers' experience modification is effective from February 1, 2000-2001. Its normal anniversary rating date is February 1. It wants to change the policy renewal to July 1, 2000, so that premium payments coincide with its fiscal year. To accomplish this, Meridian buys a new policy for the term of July 1, 2000-2001 and cancels the February policy. The February 1, 2000 modification applies until February 1, 2001. A new modification applies from February 1, 2001 until July 1, 2001. The new normal anniversary rating date begins July 1, 2001, when a new modification and rates also apply.

The previous two examples apply for single-policy risks. Other rules apply if more than one policy with varying effective dates are involved.

Why is this important? Credit and debit modifications can greatly affect the amount of workers compensation premium that a business has to pay. The experience rating procedure is designed so that a company cannot unfairly escape poor loss experience. It promotes safe workplaces by offering a financial incentive to companies that prevent worker injuries.

## The Mod Formula

It is beyond the scope of this book to go into detail on the actual mod calculation, so only a basic overview is presented, beginning with the NCCI mod calculation formula. Most states follow it or similar formulas.

### NCCI Formula

| Actual Primary Losses | + | Ballast Value | + | Weighting Value Times Actual Excess Losses | + | (1 - Weighting Value) Times Expected Excess Losses | = | Total A |
|---|---|---|---|---|---|---|---|---|
| Expected Primary Losses | + | Ballast Value | + | Weighting Value Times Expected Excess Losses | + | (1 - Weighting Value) Times Expected Excess Losses | = | Total B |

Total A, which represents the specific company being rated, is divided by Total B, which represents expected experience for the class. The mod is rounded to two places.

Each claim that goes into the calculation is divided into a primary and excess portion. *Actual primary losses* reflect an insured's claim frequency. The maximum primary value for each loss used in the calculation is $5,000. Thus, if an insured has two losses—one valued at $107,000 and one valued at $4,000—the actual primary losses used are $9,000. This represents $5,000 of the first claim and all of the $4,000 claim. This captures the frequency of losses, regardless of severity. *Actual excess losses* are total losses minus actual primary losses. In both cases, incurred losses (paid and reserve amounts) are used.

The NCCI caps the value of medical-only claims—in which there is no lost work time—at 30 percent of the actual primary and excess portions of the individual claim. Therefore, a medical-only claim valued at $7,000 would contribute only $1,500 ($5,000 x 3 percent) to the actual primary losses and $600 to actual excess losses ($2,000 x 30 percent).

Actual excess losses are weighted so that only a portion are used in determining both actual and expected excess losses. Weighting values are published by the NCCI.

Again, experience rating focuses more on the frequency of losses than on the severity. The *ballast value* helps to achieve this goal. It is a constant that is published by the NCCI. It increases as expected losses increase to offset the effect of a single large loss. The ballast value is added to both actual primary and expected primary losses.

The losses that go into the calculation are subject to limits that are set by the NCCI. There is a maximum amount that may be included for 1) an accident involving one person; or 2) an accident involving two or more individuals. The maximum values vary by state, but an example would be a per claim limit for one person of $106,500 and a multiple claim accident limit of $213,000. There also is a limit for occupational disease losses.

## Unit Statistical Plan

How is information about individual businesses gathered? The mod calculation starts with the filing of *unit statistical reports* by carriers. The reports relay premium and loss information to the appropriate bureau. Details are contained in the NCCI statistical plan manual. General familiarity with how the reporting works is important for agents and insureds because of timing issues.

The unit stat report presents a snapshot of premium and loss information at eighteen months after policy expiration and at annual intervals thereafter until three reports have been filed. Claim values on these dates are used in the mod calculation. It therefore is important to review claims *prior to the report dates* to determine whether claim reserves can be reduced and to determine other management procedures that might reduce the financial value of claims.

For example, a worker may hurt his back at work. In the first few months of the injury, the insurance company pays his medical bills of $20,0000, pays lost time wages of $8,500, sets medical reserves at $45,000, and sets lost time reserves at $52,000. The carrier believes the employee will be off work for at least a year. However, initial treatment is successful, and he returns to work much earlier than expected. It is important for the reserved amounts to be reduced to reflect this return to work *before* the unit statistical report is filed. More information on claims management is contained in Chapter 12.

## Making the Calculation

Upon receiving the statistical data about a risk, the NCCI calculates and issues the modification, which is effective on the normal anniversary rating date. At times the issuance of a modification may be delayed. In these cases a contingent or tentative modification may be attached to the policy. Once the regular mod is issued, premium adjustments are retroactive to the normal anniversary rating date.

A sample experience rating worksheet for fictitious insured Able Manufacturing is printed in Appendix B. When a worksheet is received, elements such as payroll and actual losses should be reviewed for accuracy. If errors are found a request for recalculation should be made.

## Applying the Mod

Experience mods apply to the premium that a risk develops by using an insurance company's rates in force on the effective date of the mod. The following portions of premium are *not* subject to experience modification:
- Loss constants
- Expense constants
- Policy minimum premium
- The minimum premium for coverage under Admiralty Law and the Federal Employers' Liability Act
- Premium under the National Defense Projects Rating Plan
- Seat surcharge for aircraft operation under Code 9108
- Premium under atomic energy classifications 9984 and 9985
- Premium developed by occupational disease rates for risks subject to the Federal Coal Mine Health and Safety Act

- Premium developed under three-year fixed rate policies
- Nonratable elements of manual rates
- Assigned risk surcharge premium
- Debits and credits under schedule rating
- Premium discounts based on premium size
- Premium generated for Migrant and Seasonal Agricultural Worker Protection Act coverage

The mod does apply to all other areas of premium. Once the modified premium is calculated, it is adjusted for credits, assigned risk surcharges, premium discounts, and expense concepts.

## Recalculation and Revisions

A classification of a business may be revised as the result of a change in risk operations. The experience modification is recalculated when this happens, with past payrolls reassigned to the revised classification. This could result in either a higher or lower mod, depending on the rate of the new classification.

When losses are retroactively revised, the mod also may be revised. However, the recalculation as a result of changes in losses usually is done only for one of three reasons: clerical error, payment recovery, or no payment made. Mod revisions may be requested if:

1. there is a clerical error in the original unit statistical plan card;
2. there is an uncontested recovery from a third party;
3. a claim turns out not to be compensable, or
4. there is a recovery from a special fund, such as a second injury fund.

Modifications cannot be retroactively changed simply because reserves were set too high when they were initially calculated.

When a recalculation results in a lower modification, the change is made retroactively to the policy inception date or anniversary rating date. The application of a higher recalculated modification varies depending on how long a policy has been in effect or the length of time since the anniversary rating date.

If an increase occurs during the first ninety days of a policy period, it is applied retroactively to the inception date. After the first ninety days, the increase is applied on a pro rata basis from the date the insurer endorses the policy with the new modification. If the increase is recalculated within the first ninety days after the anniversary rating date (if different from inception date) it applies retroactively to the anniversary rating date. If recalculated more than ninety days after the anniversary rating date, the mod is applied on a pro rata basis from the endorsement date.

However, a higher recalculated mod is applied retroactively to inception date if the recalculation is caused by:

- the employer failing to comply with audits or because of other faults caused by an agent or employer;
- retroactive reclassification of a risk; or
- change in ownership.

## One Risk or Two?

Company mergers and acquisitions present special situations for experience rating. After a merger, the acquired business's historical loss experience usually is transferred to the acquiring owner and excluded from the experience of the prior owner.

For example, Fabulous Footware purchases Trendy Dry Cleaners, a five-year-old company that has a modification of 1.5 because of poor claims experience. Fabulous Footware has had good loss experience and is benefiting from a modification of .75. Trendy's experience is reassigned to Fabulous. The combination of Fabulous's good experience and Trendy's poor experience results in a new modification of 1.05. The revised modification must be applied to all of Fabulous's operations, even though the types of operations differ from one another.

If Fabulous were not experience rated before the acquisition, an experience modification would be calculated using all of both company's experience. Fabulous now would have a modification that would apply to both operations.

But what if Fabulous doesn't want to be penalized for Trendy's losses? Can Fabulous keep Trendy a separate operation and thereby avoid a combined modification?

The NCCI experience rating plan, as well as those of other jurisdictions, in most instances require that only one modification be used for *all operations* of a risk. A risk is defined as either a single entity or two or more entities which qualify for combination under the plan. Two or more entities are to be combined only if:

1.  the same person, group of persons, or corporation owns more than 50 percent of each entity; or
2.  an entity owns a majority interest in another entity, which in turn owns a major interest in another entity. In this case, all the entities are combinable regardless of how many there are.

Therefore, if the owners of Fabulous, or the corporation itself, own more than 51 percent of Trendy, only one modification is used. Majority ownership is based on a majority of issued voting stock, a majority of the members if no voting stock is issued, a majority of the governing board, or participation of each general partner in the profits of a partnership. Limited partnerships are not considered when determining majority interest.

Changes of ownership also may result from:

- sale or transfer of all or a portion or an entity's ownership interests;
- sale or transfer of an entity's physical assets to another firm that takes over the business;
- formation of a new entity after an existing entity is dissolved; or
- voluntary or court-mandated establishment of a trustee or receiver.

In these cases, the experience of the prior business usually transfers to the surviving or new business. However, the prior business's loss experience may not be transferred to the new owner if: 1) there is a completely new owner; 2) there is a change in operation that results in a reclassification of the governing code; or 3) the material change in ownership includes a change in the process and hazard of the operation.

When ownership changes, the insurance company reports the details of the change to the appropriate rating organization. The information may be submitted in narrative form on the insured's letterhead and signed by an officer of the company. Or, the information may be reported by using a form entitled the Confidential Request for Information (ERM-14). Often carriers request a completed ERM-14 form from insureds when there is a question of whether entities should be combined for experience purposes. A copy of this form is reproduced in Appendix B.

## Experience Rating Summary

Experience rating embodies a simple goal within a complex process. It is designed to encourage safe working conditions by providing a financial incentive to reduce worker injuries. Companies that succeed in this reap a financial reward through a lower than average experience modification. Businesses that fail to do so are penalized with a higher than average modification. Experience rating directly affects a company's competitive economic stance.

## Schedule Rating

As noted previously, schedule rating may be used in addition to experience rating. The NCCI or other appropriate rating bureaus administer the schedule rating plans. This discussion focuses on the NCCI model.

Schedule rating credits or debits are applied *after* the experience modification. The maximum credit or debit is 25 percent. The goal of schedule rating is to reflect characteristics of a particular company that are not reflected in experience rating. NCCI rules require that schedule rating be applied to filed and approved rates *without deviations.* Deviations are discounts that are filed by carriers and applied to rates before the premium is calculated.

Schedule credits or debits are assigned for reasons such as:

- Drug free workplaces;
- Management cooperation;
- Safety devices and equipment;
- Safe work environments;
- Active employee safety committees;
- On-premises emergency medical facilities or personnel;
- Selection, training, experience, controls motivation, and supervision of employees;
- Classification peculiarities caused by technology, employee distribution, or assignment.

Carriers report the total dollar amount of schedule credits and debits they apply annually to the NCCI. Schedule credits and debits that are applied to an account must be backed up by evidence contained in the carrier's file on the account. If an insured corrects a situation that led to a debit to the carrier's satisfaction, it may be removed effective with the date that correction documentation was received by the insurer.

Thus, in addition to the effect of an experience modification, an insured's workers compensation premium may be subject to a 25 percent increase or decrease based on schedule credits.

## Why Is This Important?

As noted in the previous chapter on premium, the rates that are used for workers compensation coverage often are fairly consistent across classifications. However, businesses can directly control their premiums by preventing and managing claims to earn a lower experience mod. In addition, they can institute safety and employee training programs that enable them to qualify for schedule rating, another source of potentially lower premiums.

The opposite also is true. Both experience and schedule rating penalize businesses that fail to institute programs to prevent and manage claims. These businesses are forced to pay higher premiums for coverage that is mandated by law.

# Chapter 11

# Financial Plans

## Introduction

Workers compensation programs have what are called front and back ends. The front end is the cost at the start of the policy term. The back end is the way in which claims affect the ultimate cost. Both the front and back ends must be considered when choosing a financial plan.

The standard premium was discussed in previous chapters. It is the starting point in determining the cost of a workers compensation policy. The standard premium is amended by application of the experience modification factor, which was discussed in Chapter 10. (Some states also may tax the standard premium.) The result is called the modified standard premium, which is displayed on the policy declarations page and is considered the front end cost. The modified standard premium may be paid in a lump sum (annual premium) or in installments over the term of the policy.

Some workers compensation programs start and end with the modified standard premium. In these, there is no back end. The insured merely pays the premium, the policy is issued, claims are turned into the insurance company, and no more money changes hands between the insured and insurer unless audited payrolls differ from the estimated payrolls used at policy inception. The entire risk of the workers compensation exposure is transferred to the insurance company. Such programs are called fully insured or *guaranteed cost* plans. Only a change in payrolls or a revision in the experience modifier can generate a premium change.

The far extreme from guaranteed cost workers compensation is *self-insurance*. With self-insurance, the standard premium also is the starting point. The insured self finances the workers compensation exposure instead of buying a policy. In other words, the insured takes on the entire risk of worker injuries. Some insureds who elect self insurance do cap their exposure through the use of excess loss or stop loss insurance. Excess or stop loss insurance limits the dollar value of claims for which the self-insured business is responsible. Claim costs above the excess or stop loss point are paid by the insurance company that provides the excess loss coverage. However, for practical purposes, the exposure remains with the client. Most states require that businesses either purchase a workers compensation insurance policy or become qualified self-insurers. They cannot choose to be uninsured. In self-insured plans, the experience modifier does not affect the cost.

Another way to view this is to look at fixed costs versus variable costs. Fixed costs are those costs that do not change unless the payroll changes. Under a guaranteed cost program, the entire premium is fixed; there is no variable cost. The insured pays the premium and does not risk having to pay more if claims are worse than expected. Conversely, the insured does not have the opportunity to receive a premium return from the insurance company if claims are better than expected. After the premium is paid, the only exchange of money comes at the time of the payroll audit. If payrolls are higher than estimated at policy inception, the insured is billed for additional premium. If payrolls are lower than estimated at policy inception, the insured receives a return premium.

In a self-insured program, the fixed costs are much lower than in a guaranteed cost program. They are comprised of items such as excess premium for stop loss coverage, assessments, premium for a self-insurance bond, taxes, and service fees. They may be as low as 10 percent of the standard premium. The bulk of the costs are variable. Variable costs are comprised mainly of the cost of claims—both adjusting and paying them. The ultimate cost of a self-insured program can be much different than predicted at inception because of the impact of claims.

Market conditions, account size, and account claims history affect the type of financial plans available. When the market is soft, a greater variety of financial plans are offered even when individual account loss history is poor. When the market hardens, however, fewer options are offered and an individual company's loss history may have a greater impact on the type of financial plan available. In addition, smaller companies may not be eligible for certain financial plans. They may only be eligible for a fully insured, or guaranteed cost, program.

Between the two extremes of guaranteed cost and self insurance are a number of other methods of financing the workers compensation exposure.

This chapter examines them in terms of:

- amount of insurance purchased;
- cash flow arrangements;
- amount of fixed costs;
- amount of risk transferred to insurance company; and
- amount of collateral required.

## Types of Financial Plans

The types of financial plans that will be discussed in this chapter are guaranteed cost, standard dividend, sliding scale dividend, incurred loss retrospective rating, paid loss retrospective rating, and deductibles. Self-insurance and captive plans will not be discussed because they are individually designed and beyond the scope of this book.

Figure 4 at the end of this chapter highlights some of the major differences among seven types of financial plans.

Many workers compensation experts use premium size guidelines when deciding what type of financial plan a business should seek. Very small businesses with workers compensation premiums of $25,000 or less may not be offered any choice other than a guaranteed cost or dividend plan. Since there is no down side to a dividend plan for the insured, it is attractive to small businesses. Adverse market conditions may cause insurers to refrain from offering dividend plans to all but the best accounts, however, so businesses may be forced to purchase a guaranteed cost program.

NCCI regulations do permit companies to offer incurred loss retrospective plans to companies with premiums of $25,000 or more. Since there is the risk of paying more with a retro plan, businesses need to be sure they can financially assume that risk.

As businesses grow in size and sophistication, the types of financial plans they are offered also become more complex. Figure 1 illustrates the relative trade-off between risk and cash flow that are features of various types of plans. Larger businesses should be sure that they have adequate safety and claims management systems in place before choosing a plan that requires them to take on substantial risk. Financial stability also is considered by insurers when when they offer a workers compensation plan that has attractive cash flow.

Some professionals use a premium of $300,000 as the threshold for businesses that desire to self-insure. This is only a rule of thumb, but it is wise to remember that a certain premium size is necessary to support the management programs that are required with self insurance.

Both the qualitative and quantitative aspects of a program should be studied when choosing a plan. The quantitative aspects are the actual dollars that are expected to be spent in covering worker injuries. Qualitatively, a company may desire a specific financial program because it provides a greater opportunity for the company to influence loss control and claims adjusting. An insurer usually is more likely to coordinate these activities with the insured that is retaining more risk. It is important to remember, however, that an insurance company always retains the final decision-making authority on claims in any type of insured workers compensation program.

The way in which worker injuries are managed can greatly impact both current and future workers compensation costs. Because of this, close attention to cost and program management must be paid when trying to understand and select an appropriate workers compensation program. The various types of plans can be placed on a continuum of insurance options. This continuum places the program factors on a relative scale of amount of insurance, cash flow, fixed costs, risk, and collateral requirements. As illustrated in the chart below, guaranteed cost programs generally include the most insurance and least risk. Cash flow management is low or non-existent. At the other end of the continuum is self-insurance, which features the least insurance, best cash flow management, and lowest fixed costs. In exchange for these pluses, a self-insured company takes on the most risk and highest collateral requirement. Of course, the fixed cost structures of each program vary depending upon market conditions.

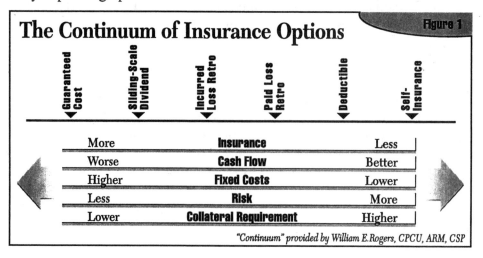

# The Continuum of Insurance Options

Figure 1

| Guaranteed Cost | Sliding-Scale Dividend | Incurred Loss Retro | Paid Loss Retro | Deductible | Self-Insurance |
|---|---|---|---|---|---|

| More | Insurance | Less |
| Worse | Cash Flow | Better |
| Higher | Fixed Costs | Lower |
| Less | Risk | More |
| Lower | Collateral Requirement | Higher |

*"Continuum" provided by William E. Rogers, CPCU, ARM, CSP*

## Guaranteed Cost Plans

A workers compensation policy with a fixed or guaranteed cost premium is the most conservative and the easiest to understand. Such programs are stable in regard to cost. A company that chooses a guaranteed cost plan knows what worker injuries will cost at policy inception because the policy premium *is* the cost. The premium varies only as a factor of payroll and experience modifier, if applicable. It does not vary directly as the result of loss experience and cannot be increased retrospectively.

The guaranteed cost premium is the manual, or standard, premium. If an account qualifies for an experience modifier, it is applied to the standard premium. The standard premium calculation is discussed in Chapter 9. The experience modifier is discussed in Chapter 10. The guaranteed cost program is the starting point for all workers compensation programs and can be reduced by discounts, dividends, and deductibles or increased by loss or expense constants. Even though it is the easiest to understand, it may not be the most desirable—or even available in the marketplace.

## Dividend Plans

These plans are designed so that an insured may receive a dividend if worker injuries are less expensive than anticipated. They are designed to reward companies that do a good job in preventing and managing worker injuries. The dividend may be based on the loss experience of a particular group to which the insured belongs or of the individual insured. In group dividend plans, the claims experience of the entire group is compiled. If the insurer has made a profit on the group, a dividend may be declared. In like fashion, individual dividends are determined based on the amount of losses the individual company incurs.

Dividends are never guaranteed. They are payable only upon declaration of the insurer's board of directors. If declared, they are paid at various intervals after the policy expires, sometimes in a lump sum and sometimes in a series of payments. Dividends usually are not computed earlier than twelve months or more after policy expiration. The details on how and when the dividend is due should be provided before policy inception.

In addition, policies with back-end dividend plans are subject to experience rating. Therefore, if a company qualifies for an experience modifier, it is used to develop the standard premium. Stock and/or mutual company discounts also are applied to policies that offer a back-end dividend.

## Standard Dividend Plans

A standard or flat dividend, if declared, is paid a year or more after a policy expires. They are most often used with affinity or group programs. Affinity programs are designed around a type of business. For example, a trade group of manufacturers, grocery stores, schools, or other business type may develop a workers compensation group program that is open to association members. Since the group represents a large amount of premium, insurers may be willing to offer a dividend plan to its members. Even though an insured receives the benefit of a possible dividend, the insured will not have to pay additional premium—aside from additional premium that may be developed in the payroll audit. An exception exists for assessable insurance policies issued by an assessable mutual insurance company or reciprocal.

Dividend plans work because insureds are rewarded when the insurer makes an underwriting profit on a homogeneous group of accounts. Since the insured does not risk having to pay more premium in the event of bad losses, the potential return is lower than in riskier plans. There is a trade-off between risk and potential benefit.

For example, an association of manufacturers may go to one carrier to purchase workers compensation insurance. Individual group members are underwritten separately, and the amount of premium for each is reviewed as a whole to provide the insurer with an incentive to write the coverage. Individual workers compensation policies are issued to each group member, and each pays its own premium. After the policies expire, the claims experience of all members is combined to determine whether an underwriting profit was made. If so, the insurer may declare a dividend. However, if claims costs are higher than a predetermined amount, a dividend is not possible.

Group or affinity programs often are used when coverage is hard to obtain, especially when the workers compensation premium of individual group members is relatively low. An insurance company may not be interested in taking the risk of insuring a small manufacturer, which generates only $15,000 of premium but has the potential of thousands of dollars of losses. However, if a number of small companies solicit coverage as a group, the combined premium often is large enough to interest several insurers. Small companies may join the group so that they can qualify for a potential dividend.

There are times when insurance companies will offer a group dividend to an entire group, which is computed based on the experience of the group as a whole, as well as individual dividends to members, which are computed on the experience of the member. In these types of programs, a group member is eligible to receive two dividends.

## Sliding Scale Dividends

The next type of dividend plan is tied directly to the underwriting results of individual insureds. Instead of relying on group experience, an individual company stands on its own claims experience for purposes of dividend calculation. These are called sliding scale dividend plans. They start with the expectations of a particular loss ratio. Insureds who develop a lower loss ratio may be rewarded with a dividend. Those who develop a higher than expected loss ratio lose the dividend opportunity.

For example, a plan might assume that the incurred loss ratio for a manufacturer will be 65 percent. The incurred loss ratio is determined by dividing incurred losses by the earned premium. Incurred losses include both paid and reserved claim amounts. If the loss ratio is less than 65 percent, a dividend may be declared. If the loss ratio is higher than 65 percent, the insured is not responsible to pay more premium; the insurance company has to absorb the excess losses. However, the company forfeits the dividend. This type of plan provides a financial incentive to prevent worker injuries and to manage the claims that do occur.

Sliding scale dividend plans are usually written for either one or three years. A three-year plan can be written in either of two ways. Under the first approach, a computation is made at the end of the first, second, third, and succeeding years. Partial dividends may be paid at each computation. However, starting with the second year, the computation includes all prior years up to a maximum of three years. With the second approach, the computation is not made until the end of the third year. Some three-year plans may include a *recapture* provision, which requires the insured to pay back prior-year dividends if, at subsequent valuations during the three years of losses, claims deteriorate.

In a one-year plan, losses are valued as of a predetermined date, such as at twelve or eighteen months after policy expiration. If the loss ratio is less than a predetermined percentage, a dividend may be paid. The amount of the dividend *slides* with the loss ratio, subject to a maximum possible dividend. For example, a sliding scale plan could be written so that the insured gets 75 percent of the savings if the account's loss ratio is less than the expected 60 percent but greater than or equal to 35 percent. If the loss ratio is less than 35 percent, it is treated as if the loss ratio were 35 percent.

The formula for this plan would be

Dividend =    .75 x (.60 - actual loss ratio) x Premium

The actual loss ratio used can be no lower than 35 percent.

Consider three cases. All three are based on the following assumptions:

1.    A one-year sliding scale dividend plan is used.
2.    The audited premium is $100,000.
3.    The expected loss ratio is 60 percent (the insurer expects $60,000 in losses).
4.    The dividend is based on 75 percent of the savings subject to a minimum usable loss ratio of 35 percent.

In the first example, ABC Company has $50,000 of losses, which translates into a 50 percent loss ratio ($50,000 of incurred losses divided by $100,000 premium). ABC earns a dividend of $7,500, which is 75 percent times the difference between the expected loss ratio of 60 percent and the actual loss ratio of 50 percent, times the premium. The formula is 75 percent x (60 percent - 50 percent) x $100,000, which equals a dividend of $7,500.

In the second example, ABC has $65,000 in losses or a 65 percent loss ratio. Since the loss ratio is more than 60 percent, no dividend is earned.

In the third example, ABC has $30,000 in losses, which is a 30 percent loss ratio. The formula for ABC's dividend would be

Dividend =    75 percent x (60 percent - 30 percent) x $100,000
Dividend =    $22,500

However, since the lowest loss ratio that can be used in this plan is 35 percent, ABC only receives a dividend of $18,750. The 35 percent loss ratio must be used in place of the actual 30 percent earned, for a calculation as follows:

Dividend =    75 percent x (60 percent - *35 percent*) x $100,000
Dividend =    $18,750

This sliding scale dividend plan also can be illustrated as:

## Estimated Dividend Display

## Audited Premium of $100,000

| Loss Ratio | Losses | Dividend | Net Premium |
|---|---|---|---|
| 60% + | $60,000 + | $0 | $100,000 |
| 55% | $55,000 | $3,750 | $96,250 |
| 50% | $50,000 | $7,500 | $92,500 |
| 45% | $45,000 | $11,250 | $88,750 |
| 40% | $40,000 | $15,000 | $85,000 |
| 35% | $35,000 | $18,750 | $81,250 |
| Less than 35% | Less than $35,000 | $18,750 | $81,250 |

As shown, the maximum dividend possible with a $100,000 premium is $18,750.

Sliding scale plans are popular because the account can benefit from better than expected losses without the threat of additional premium if losses are worse than expected. These plans are not often available to insureds with poor or fluctuating loss histories because no risk, and only an opportunity to gain, is transferred to the insured. Keep Figure 1 in mind. A sliding scale dividend plan is to the right of a guaranteed cost plan because the insured is beginning to take on financial responsibility for preventing and managing its own claims.

## Retrospective Rating Plans

Retrospective rating rewards companies that have below average losses and penalizes those with above average losses in the policy year *in which the claims occurred*. The premium for expired policies is adjusted as claims develop and mature. Workers compensation claims often have long tails. An accident may occur during the policy term and remain open for several years—until the worker is completely healed and back to work or she is placed in some type of permanent disability program. Claims experience—both good and bad—affects the ultimate cost of the policy during which the claims occurred.

Under a retrospectively rated plan, an insured is affected by losses in two ways. First, its current retrospective policy premium is adjusted upward or downward based on claims that occur in that policy year. Second, its future experience modifier is reduced if losses are lower than expected. The future modifier is increased if losses are higher than expected. This double benefit or penalty occurs because experience rating is used in conjunction with retro rating. However, the *impact* of the experience modifier is less with a retro policy than with a guaranteed cost policy. The effect of the modifier is included only in the fixed cost portion of the premium and not in its variable costs.

There are two basic types of retro plans:

- Incurred loss retrospective rating plans
- Paid loss retrospective rating plans

There are any number of hybrid combinations of plans. However, only these two types are discussed in this book. The information on incurred loss retro rating is based on the National Council on Compensation Insurance (NCCI) retro rating system. States that do not belong to the NCCI issue their own retro regulations. However, for practical purposes, the NCCI program provides a general context that may be applied to non-NCCI states. In addition, the discussion will focus on the NCCI one-year incurred loss retro plan, even though three-year and multiple lines plans also are available.

A retro plan utilizes a simple concept. Insureds pay in premium during the policy term. The premium is used to issue the policy and operate the program, as well as to pay for claims adjusting and payment. Starting at six months after policy expiration, claims are reviewed. If the program operating (fixed) costs and claims (variable) costs are lower than the amount paid in, the insured receives a retrospective return premium. If they are higher than the amount paid in, the insured is billed a retrospective additional premium. Retro plans are evaluated six months after the end of the policy period (eighteen months from inception) and in twelve-month intervals thereafter. For an annual policy, the evaluation dates would be eighteen, thirty, forty-two, fifty-four months, etc., after policy inception.

In an incurred loss plan, both paid and reserved claims are included when the retro premium is calculated. Because of this, the insured is ultimately responsible for its own claims. This can lead to better loss prevention and claims management, which usually means lower total costs. Insureds may seek an incurred loss plan because it offers an opportunity to lower the ultimate premium substantially when claim costs are controlled.

Conversely, insurers may be willing to offer only a retro plan to insureds with poor claims experience for the same reason: the insured ultimately is charged for its losses. The possible gain of a lower premium is balanced against the risk that claims will be bad, which would result in a higher premium.

Companies qualify for a one-year retrospective rating plan if their estimated modified standard premium is at least $25,000. This estimated standard premium may include workers compensation and other casualty insurance lines. However, when a combined lines retro is used, the Insurance Services Office (ISO) retrospective rating plan should be consulted.

Even though a minimum $25,000 of modified standard premium is the NCCI threshold, many companies require a higher premium.

## Retrospective Rating Formula

The retrospective rating premium formula is as follows:

Retrospective Premium = [(Basic Factor x Standard Premium) + (Losses x Loss Conversion Factor)] x Tax Multiplier

The retro premium is limited by minimum and maximum premiums.

The *basic factor (BF)* is the percentage standard premium that is needed to issue the policy and operate the program. It includes insurer underwriting expenses; producer commission, if applicable; insurance charges; and profit. The basic factor usually ranges from .15 to .35, depending upon the size of the risk, the amount of insurance being provided, and other factors in the plan. The basic factor multiplied by the standard premium develops the *basic premium.*

The *loss conversion factor (LCF)* is a percentage that represents the cost to adjust claims. It usually ranges from .08 to .15 of losses. At times, adjusting costs are represented by a dollar figure per type of claim instead of a percentage. For purposes of this discussion, a percentage LCF is used. The LCF is added to the total value of claims, which then are referred to as *converted losses.* The LCF reflects general claims adjusting costs. Unusual adjusting costs—such as special surveillance and expert witness testimony—may be allocated to specific claims. These are called *allocated loss adjusting expenses (ALAE).* ALAE are added to the converted losses, but they are not subject to the LCF.

The *tax multiplier (TM)* is the average of the taxes, fees, and assessments that apply to the account. In general, tax multipliers fall in the range of 1.04 to 1.06.

Retrospective premiums are limited by *minimum* and *maximum* premiums. The retro premium can never fall below the minimum premium, regardless of how good the loss experience is. This is because the insurance company must be able to recover its program costs. The maximum premium ensures that the risk is not subject to unlimited losses. The insured may choose to buy coverage that limits individual losses in addition to the overall premium limit provided by the maximum. This is called purchasing *loss limitations* or *loss limits*.

Retro plans are not eligible for insurer premium discounts. This is because premium discounts are used to lower the expense portion of the guaranteed cost premium. Since retro plan operating expenses are covered by the basic premium, operating costs are, in theory, already minimized.

The basic and loss conversion factors, as well as the minimum and maximum premiums, are set through negotiation between the insured and insurer. Therefore, there can be major differences in the final amount of the retro premium among insurance companies. It is important to monitor the financial implications of a retro plan through the entire time it remains open.

## Excess Loss Premium

If the standard premium that is subject to retro rating is at least $100,000, insureds may elect to purchase *excess loss* coverage. Excess loss coverage limits the amount of incurred loss arising from one accident that will be included in the retro premium calculation. Excess loss coverage also is referred to as buying a loss limit or limitation.

For example, a retro plan may incorporate only the first $100,000 in cost of each worker accident in the claims portion of the retro formula. This type of plan caps losses at $100,000 per accident. Only the first $100,000 of incurred loss from each accident is used in the retro premium formula. The premium for the statutory coverage above the loss limit of $100,000 is not subject to retrospective rating. It is called the *excess loss premium or nonsubject premium.* The nonsubject premium does not fluctuate with losses; it is simply added to the retro premium at the end of the calculation. The workers compensation retrospective rating endorsement, which is attached to the policy, shows the subject and nonsubject premiums separately.

## How a Retro Works

The following illustrates the way in which a retro works by discussing four policies, all of which are written on one-year retrospective plans. Each of the policies has:

- modified standard premium of $100,000;
- maximum premium of $140,000; and
- minimum premium of $70,000.

Figure 2 illustrates how the first adjustment of each policy, made at six months after expiration, generates different results for each policy.

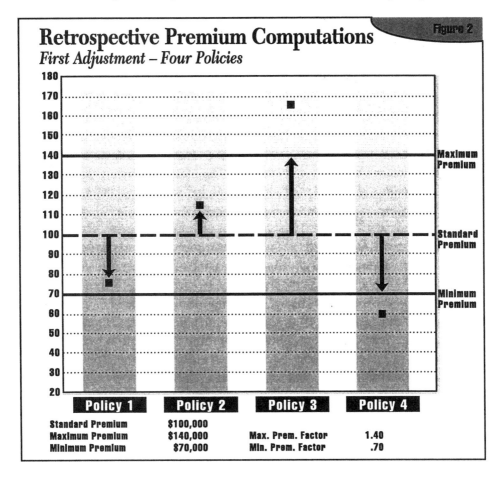

In these policies, the entire modified standard premium of $100,000 was paid to the insurance company during the policy term. Thus, retro adjustments were made on the basis of a premium pay-in of $100,000.

As discussed previously, workers compensation claims often take a significant amount of time to mature and develop to maximum potential. Over a period of years a claim may increase or decrease in value as the worker undergoes continuing treatment or goes back to work. Consequently, the losses that are used in annual retro calculations may differ significantly from those used at the first adjustment.

As shown in Figure 2, the first adjustment for Policy 1 resulted in a retro premium of $80,000. Therefore, $20,000 was returned to the insured. The first adjustment for Policy 2 produced a retro premium of $110,000, so the insured was billed $10,000 additional premium. Policy 3 generated a premium of $166,000 at the first adjustment because of several large claims. Since the program includes a maximum premium of $140,000, the insured was billed only $40,000. Policy 4 would generate a return premium of $45,000 if there were no minimum premium. Lower than expected claims produced a retrospectively adjusted premium of only $55,000. The insured only received a return premium of $30,000 because $70,000 is the minimum premium.

However, the premium for each of these policies continues to be adjusted annually based in the development of losses. To illustrate this refer to Figure 3, which charts the first four retro adjustments, which are issued at intervals of eighteen, thirty, forty-two, and fifty-four months after policy inception.

Policy 1 generated a $20,000 return premium at the first adjustment. At the end of thirty months (second adjustment), the retro premium was recalculated at $115,000 because several claims deteriorated. The insured is not only required to pay the difference between the standard premium ($100,000) and the retro premium ($115,000), but it also must *repay* the $20,000 return it received at the first adjustment. Thus, the premium billing at thirty months is for $35,000. At the end of forty-two months, claims continue to deteriorate, and the retro premium increases to $165,000. The insured is billed $25,000 because the $165,000 exceeds the maximum $140,000 premium. The fourth computation produces a retro premium of $125,000, because several claims were resolved at costs lower than anticipated. The insured therefore is returned $15,000 ($125,000 less $140,000 paid to date).

These adjustments continue until all claims are closed or the insured and insurer mutually agree to close the plan. It is not unusual for retro programs to remain open for five or more years, especially in long-term exposures such as workers compensation.

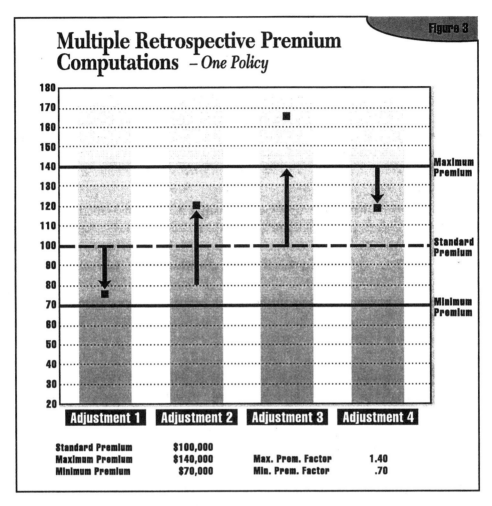

## Optional Retro Premium Components

The basic retrospective premium formula discussed previously does not include two optional elements that may be added separately to a retro plan. They are excess loss premiums and retrospective development factors. The *excess loss premium* pays for stop loss or loss limitation insurance, which was mentioned. The excess loss premium may be included within the basic premium. However, it also may be shown as a separate charge, which is outside the retro adjustment.

If a plan is written with a per accident loss limit of $100,000, only the first $100,000 in claim costs arising from each accident is used in the retro premium calculation. Such excess loss coverage stabilizes retro plans by dampening the effect of large losses. For example, three employees might be seriously injured in an industrial accident. The total cost of all three injuries might run into the hundreds of thousands of dollars. If a $100,000 per accident loss limit were purchased, only the first $100,000 of all claims arising from the one accident would be included in the retro adjustment. If a $100,000 *per claim* loss limit had been chosen, the first $100,000 cost of each worker's injuries, or $300,000, would be included in losses used in the retro adjustment.

The purpose of the *retrospective development premium* is to smooth out some of the fluctuations that often occur between the first and subsequent retro adjustments; it stabilizes the retro premium over time. The *retrospective development premium* reduces the likelihood that the insured will receive a large premium return at the first calculation, which likely will have to be repaid to the insurer at subsequent calculations.

## Audit vs. Retro Calculation

The terms *premium audit* and *premium calculation and adjustment* often are confused, but they are decidedly different calculations. The premium audit always precedes the retro premium computation and adjustment. Assume that a workers compensation risk is being retrospectively rated. The rate is applied to each $100 of payroll. The standard premium is equal to payroll divided by 100, multiplied by the manual rate and experience modification factor. The initial premium is merely an estimate, but it is the amount paid to the insurer before or during the policy term. The actual modified standard premium is determined at the premium audit. At policy expiration, the insurance company audits the payrolls. If the payroll is more than estimated, an additional premium is charged. If less, a refund is made. This *audited modified standard premium* then is used as the pay-in amount at the first retro adjustment.

## Retro Policy Cancellation

If an insured goes out of business, a one-year retro plan is cancelled as follows:

1.  the modified standard premium is calculated on a pro rata basis; and

2.  the retrospective premium then is calculated using the pro rata modified standard premium.

The minimum and maximum premium factors are applied to the pro rata modified standard premium. If the minimum and maximum factors were .50 and 1.5 respectively, they would be multiplied against the modified standard premium to develop the dollar amount of the minimum and maximum on the pro rata cancellation.

However, insureds who cancel a retro plan for reasons other than going out of business are penalized to discourage them from bailing out of a retro plan that is not going well. The process in this case is:

1.    the premium for the policy is calculated on a short-rate basis; and

2.    the retrospective premium is calculated using the short-rate premium.

The short-rate is calculated by taking the partial premium for the period the plan was in effect, extending it for a full year, and then multiplying the result times the short-rate factor. The short-rate premium is used as the minimum premium. In addition, the annualized standard premium, rather than the short-rate premium, is used as the basis for computing the maximum premium. This serves as an additional deterrent to canceling the policy under adverse loss conditions.

## Retrospective Rating Forms

Insureds must sign an election form indicating that they are aware of selecting a retro rating plan. An election form usually contains the following information: name of insured; date plan takes effect; formula factors (basic premium factor, minimum premium factor, maximum premium factor, loss conversion factor, tax multiplier, and retrospective development factor if applicable); loss limitations and excess loss premium factor if applicable; signature of insured; date election form signed; and policies covered under the plan. Retrospective rating is included in a policy by attaching a retrospective endorsement. These are described in Chapter 6.

## Incurred Loss vs. Paid Loss Plans

The main difference between an incurred loss and paid loss plan is the type of claims included in the calculations. The major benefit with a paid loss plan lies in cash flow; the money that is paid in to the insurer is based on the amount of paid claims.

In a paid loss plan, the insured pays the insurer a deposit premium and sets up a claims fund at the beginning of the year. The deposit premium is similar to the basic premium in an incurred loss plan; it is designed to cover insurer expenses and profit. The claims fund is established so that the insurer can pay claims as they come due. The insured is required to replenish the claims fund as the insurance company uses it to pay claims. The difference between this *pay-in amount* and the estimated standard premium usually must be posted in collateral.

It can take many years for a paid loss plan to close. Therefore, the insured is expected to pay claims long after a policy has expired. Collateral is required as a financial guarantee that future claims will be funded. The collateral often is in the form of a letter of credit or cash escrow account, but some insurers will accept other types of assets as collateral.

At regular intervals, incurred losses are reviewed and an incurred loss retrospective premium is calculated. The paid-in premium and paid losses are subtracted from the incurred loss premium. This difference is used to determine whether the required collateral should be adjusted to guarantee the payment of future claim bills. Thus, the collateral may be adjusted at the date of the annual retrospective rating calculations.

## Deductible Plans

Deductibles are used in some states for workers compensation and employers liability policies. The NCCI deductible endorsement is described in Chapter 6. Deductibles may be applicable to medical payments, indemnity payments, or both. Exhaustive credit checks usually are conducted before an insured is offered a deductible plan. This is because, under a deductible plan, the insurance company usually pays claims and then seeks reimbursement from the insured. The insured's credit worthiness thus becomes very important.

There are state-specific guidelines for deductible programs, so individual state regulations should be reviewed for specific information.

Deductibles can serve two purposes. Small deductibles are used to eliminate nuisance claims. Large deductibles are designed to offer the insured a method for increasing its retention without incurring unlimited liability and without having to handle claims, as it would under a self-insured retention. However, many insureds do negotiate with insurers to have independent companies adjust their claims under a large deductible program. One of the original incentives for large deductible programs was in the area of taxation. Since the deductible amount of claims is not actually *premium*, premium taxes and assessments were not levied against it. This offered some tax relief to insureds. However, some states have revised their taxation so that this incentive may no longer apply.

Many insurers sell large deductible plans to large companies. The deductible usually ranges from $100,000 to $1,000,000 per accident. Aggregate coverage for losses falling within the deductible layer usually is available.

The set-up of a large deductible plan is similar to the paid loss retrospective rating plan discussed previously. The insured pays a deductible premium and sets up an escrow account with funds adequate to pay the deductible portion of expected claims for a sixty to ninety-day period. Additionally, the insured is billed every month for actual payments that fall within the deductible layer. The amount of collateral required is based on estimated losses and the insured's financial condition.

As with the paid loss retro plan, the initial pay-in is substantially less than the full estimated standard premium, which is collected up-front in an incurred loss retro program. Even though the insured may have to post collateral with both paid loss and incurred loss plans, cash flow is superior to other programs.

Among the various advantages of a large deductible program are the following:

- In some states the insured's premium and other expenses are lower because, as the deductible increases, the corresponding premium falls, along with the taxes, fees, and assessments that are a function of premium.
- The insured may retain the investment income on the collateral and claims escrow funds.
- The insured realizes immediate benefits from favorable loss experience with some protection against catastrophic losses.
- A large deductible plan offers superior cash flow.
- Fixed costs (deposit premium) usually are lower than with other plans.
- The insured often retains the insurance company's administrative and claims services.
- Many insurance companies permit insureds to have a say in loss control and claims management. Some may permit the insured to hire independent loss control and claims management companies, rather than using the insurance company's personnel.

There also are negative features to large deductible plans. These include:

- A large deductible plan creates an additional administrative burden for the insured.
- The insurer still has ultimate control of claims management unless arrangements are made so that an outside firm—third party adjuster—is used to handle claims.
- The insured is limited to the services offered by the insurer unless it agrees to unbundle claims management.
- Letters of credit may be difficult to obtain or expensive for highly leveraged companies.
- Unfavorable loss experience can have a great impact on costs, and ultimate costs may be difficult to calculate unless an aggregate is purchased.
- Reserves for future loss payments are not tax deductible until the losses actually are paid, while *premiums* are deductible when paid.

## Option Evaluation Form

| Evaluation Questions | Guaranteed Cost Plan | Standard Dividend Plan | Sliding Scale Dividend Plan |
|---|---|---|---|
| 1  Is this type of plan auditable? | Yes | Yes | Yes |
| **Cash Flow** | | | |
| 2  Can costs other than audit results be fixed in advance? | Yes | Yes | Yes |
| 3  If losses are good, do I get money back? | No | Yes | Yes |
| 4  If losses are bad, do I have to pay more money? | No | No | No |
| 5  Are all program costs paid in the first year of the program? | Yes | Yes | Yes |
| 6  Are calculations made on an incurred loss or paid loss basis? | N/A | Incurred | Incurred |
| 7  Who earns interest income? | Insurer | Insurer | Insurer |
| 8  Can any of the program costs be deferred? | Possible | Possible | Possible |
| 9  Is additional up-front cash required to set up program? | No | No | No |
| **Rating** | | | |
| 10  Is there potential for a dividend payment? | No | Yes | Yes |
| 11  Is price subject to negotiation? | No | No | No |
| 12  Is program easy to understand? | Yes | Yes | Yes |
| 13  Does an expense discount apply? | Yes | Yes | Yes |
| 14  Is composite rating possible? | Yes | Yes | Yes |
| 15  Is a compensating balance arrangement possible? | N/A | N/A | N/A |
| **Taxes & Assessments** | | | |
| 16  Does insured pay full premium taxes? | Yes | Yes | Yes |
| 17  Are costs tax deductible? | Yes | Yes | Yes |
| 18  Are residual market loadings avoided? | No | No | No |
| 19  Are there other assessments? | Included in premium | | |
| **Losses** | | | |
| 20  Does insured share risk with insurer? | No | No | No |
| 21  Are loss limitations available? | N/A | N/A | N/A |
| 22  How important is loss reserving? | Not important | Somewhat important | Somewhat important |
| **Services** | | | |
| 23  How much control do I have over how the program is managed? | No control | No control | No control |
| 24  Who has the final say on how claims are managed? | Insurer | Insurer | Insurer |
| 25  How easy will it be for me to customize loss control efforts? | Difficult | Difficult | Difficult |
| 26  Can services be unbundled? | No | No | No |
| 27  Will I need an internal staff to manage the program? | No | No | No |
| 28  Is additional record keeping needed? | No | No | No |
| **General Considerations** | | | |
| 29  How much do market conditions impact this program? | Great impact | | |
| 30  Does the program provide a buffer between my company and third parties? | Yes | Yes | Yes |
| 31  In general, how flexible is the plan? | Inflexible | Inflexible | Inflexible |
| 32  Does the plan encourage loss control? | No | Minimally | Minimally |
| 33  Is firm's credit worthiness an important factor? | No | No | No |
| 34  How hard is it to move away from this type of program? | Easy | Easy | Easy |

# Option Evaluation Form

Figure 4

| Evaluation Questions | Incurred Loss Retrospective Rating Plan | Paid Loss Retrospective Rating Plan |
|---|---|---|
| 1  Is this type of plan auditable? | Yes | Yes |
| **Cash Flow** | | |
| 2  Can costs other than audit results be fixed in advance? | No | No |
| 3  If losses are good, do I get money back? | Yes | Possible/Collerateral |
| 4  If losses are bad, do I have to pay more money? | Yes | Yes |
| 5  Are all program costs paid in the first year of the program? | No | No |
| 6  Are calculations made on an incurred loss or paid loss basis? | Incurred | Paid |
| 7  Who earns interest income? | Insurer | Negotiable |
| 8  Can any of the program costs be deferred? | Yes | Yes |
| 9  Is additional up-front cash required to set up program? | No | Yes, loss fund |
| **Rating** | | |
| 10  Is there potential for a dividend payment? | N/A | N/A |
| 11  Is price subject to negotiation? | Yes | Yes |
| 12  Is program easy to understand? | May be difficult | May be difficult |
| 13  Does an expense discount apply? | No | No |
| 14  Is composite rating possible? | Yes | Yes |
| 15  Is a compensating balance arrangement possible? | N/A | Yes |
| **Taxes & Assessments** | | |
| 16  Does insured pay full premium taxes? | Yes | Yes |
| 17  Are costs tax deductible? | Yes | Yes/STR |
| 18  Are residual market loadings avoided? | No | No |
| 19  Are there other assessments? | Included in premium | |
| **Losses** | | |
| 20  Does insured share risk with insurer? | Yes | Yes |
| 21  Are loss limitations available? | Yes | Yes |
| 22  How important is loss reserving? | Extremely important | Very important |
| **Services** | | |
| 23  How much control do I have over how the program is managed? | Fair control | Fair control |
| 24  Who has the final say on how claims are managed? | Consultative/Insurer | |
| 25  How easy will it be for me to customize loss control efforts? | Negotiable | Negotiable |
| 26  Can services be unbundled? | Sometimes | Sometimes |
| 27  Will I need an internal staff to manage the program? | Possibly | Possibly |
| 28  Is additional record keeping needed? | Yes | Yes |
| **General Considerations** | | |
| 29  How much do market conditions impact this program? | Minimal impact | |
| 30  Does the program provide a buffer between my company and third parties? | Yes | Yes |
| 31  In general, how flexible is the plan? | Minimally flexible | Fairly flexible |
| 32  Does the plan encourage loss control? | Yes | Yes |
| 33  Is firm's credit worthiness an important factor? | Possibly | Yes |
| 34  How hard is it to move away from this type of program? | Difficult | Difficult |

# Option Evaluation Form

Figure 4

| Evaluation Questions | Large Deductible Plan | Self-Insured Retention Plan |
|---|---|---|
| 1  Is this type of plan auditable? | Yes | Yes |
| **Cash Flow** | | |
| 2  Can costs other than audit results be fixed in advance? | No | No |
| 3  If losses are good, do I get money back? | Possible/Collerateral | |
| 4  If losses are bad, do I have to pay more money? | Yes | Yes |
| 5  Are all program costs paid in the first year of the program? | No | No |
| 6  Are calculations made on an incurred loss or paid loss basis? | Variable | Variable |
| 7  Who earns interest income? | Negotiable | Negotiable |
| 8  Can any of the program costs be deferred? | Yes | Yes |
| 9  Is additional up-front cash required to set up program? | Yes, loss fund | Yes, loss fund |
| **Rating** | | |
| 10  Is there potential for a dividend payment? | N/A | N/A |
| 11  Is price subject to negotiation? | Yes | Yes |
| 12  Is program easy to understand? | May be difficult | May be difficult |
| 13  Does an expense discount apply? | Yes | Yes |
| 14  Is composite rating possible? | Yes | Yes |
| 15  Is a compensating balance arrangement possible? | Yes | Yes |
| **Taxes & Assessments** | | |
| 16  Does insured pay full premium taxes? | Yes/STR | Yes/STR |
| 17  Are costs tax deductible? | Yes/STR | Yes/STR |
| 18  Are residual market loadings avoided? | May be reduced | |
| 19  Are there other assessments? | May be reduced | |
| **Losses** | | |
| 20  Does insured share risk with insurer? | Yes | Yes |
| 21  Are loss limitations available? | Yes | Yes |
| 22  How important is loss reserving? | Very important | Very important |
| **Services** | | |
| 23  How much control do I have over how the program is managed? | Good control | Good control |
| 24  Who has the final say on how claims are managed? | Consultative/Insurer | |
| 25  How easy will it be for me to customize loss control efforts? | Negotiable | Negotiable |
| 26  Can services be unbundled? | Sometimes | Usually |
| 27  Will I need an internal staff to manage the program? | Possibly | Possibly |
| 28  Is additional record keeping needed? | Yes | Yes |
| **General Considerations** | | |
| 29  How much do market conditions impact this program? | Minimal impact | |
| 30  Does the program provide a buffer between my company and third parties? | Yes | Yes |
| 31  In general, how flexible is the plan? | Fairly flexible | Fairly flexible |
| 32  Does the plan encourage loss control? | Yes | Yes |
| 33  Is firm's credit worthiness an important factor? | Yes | Yes |
| 34  How hard is it to move away from this type of program? | Difficult | Difficult |

# Chapter 12

# Cost Management Issues

## Introduction

Workers compensation is much more than an insurance policy. It is a system that balances on the premise that injured workers will be taken care of regardless of fault. In exchange, workers give up the right to sue their employers for these injuries. Almost all states require most employers to either carry workers compensation insurance or become qualified workers compensation self-insurers.

Because of this, workers compensation costs directly affect the bottom line of nearly all American businesses. Controlling this bottom line cost gives employers a financial incentive to prevent worker injuries from happening and to manage those that do.

Financial incentives obviously are not the only reason for promoting a well-run workers compensation program. No amount of insurance will ever pay for the cost of lost worker productivity and experience that is incurred when an employee is injured on the job. No amount of insurance will ever adequately compensate a family for the loss or permanent disability of a father or mother.

However, financial incentives do present a measurable reason to maintain safe workplaces. The system financially rewards those companies that are able to prevent or decrease the severity of claims with lower premiums. The system penalizes those that fail to do so.

The rewards and penalties can be great. In Chapter 10 we illustrated the difference in premium between a company with a 1.25 modification and its competitor, which had earned a .85 mod. As premiums grow, the financial incentives become more prominent.

Take two supermarkets as examples. Each averages an unmodified standard premium of $100,000. The first supermarket has a modifier of 1.15; its competitor has managed claims and earned a mod of .85. In addition, both are written on sliding scale dividend plans.

To begin with, Supermarket ABC pays $115,000 in premium because of its 1.15 debit modifier. Supermarket XYZ only pays $85,000 because of its credit mod of .85. During the dividend term, Supermarket ABC has poor claims experience. It does not qualify for a dividend, so its premium remains at $115,000. Supermarket XYZ has few claims and qualifies for a $15,000 dividend. Its ultimate cost is $70,000. The difference in effect to the two supermarkets' bottom lines is $45,000. This difference becomes exacerbated as premiums grow and as more complex financial plans are compared.

This chapter focuses on programs that encourage employers, their managers, and their employees to aggressively manage the workers compensation claims that do happen. The critical element in all of them is a commitment by senior management. Absence of this commitment may not doom the programs to failure, but it certainly makes them less likely to succeed.

This work does not attempt to address workplace safety engineering; that subject is well beyond the scope of this guide. It does, however, present ideas on how claims can be managed so that workers recover and return to work as quickly as possible. There is also some information on programs that award managers and employees for improving their loss records.

## Managing Loss Reserves

Managing claim reserves is perhaps the most important financial mission in a workers compensation program. As discussed in both Chapters 10 and 11, the value of both paid and reserved claims impacts ultimate costs. Obviously, nothing can be done about claim payments already made. However, reserves should be managed because they affect both the experience modification and various workers compensation financial plans. Since reserves represent dollars earmarked for expected future payment, they can increase or decrease depending on how a claim plays out over its lifetime.

Credible data is necessary to manage loss reserves. Loss runs showing—at a minimum—date of loss, date reported, claimant's name, injury type, paid and reserved amounts of medical, paid and reserved amounts of indemnity, and allocated loss adjustment expenses, if applicable, should be obtained on a regular basis from the insurer. If the insured has a high frequency of compensation claims, loss runs should be reviewed on a monthly or quarterly basis. In low frequency insureds, loss runs may be reviewed only once or twice a year. Regardless of whether the account has a high frequency of claims or not, loss runs should be reviewed on an annual basis at least three months *before* the unit statistical report is to be filed. (Information on the unit statistical report is contained in Chapter 10.)

Why the pre-unit-stat review? Claims data is sent by the insurer to the appropriate bureau six months after policy expiration for use in calculating the experience modification. Losses should be reviewed at least three months prior to this date so that the insured has some time to address issues that may lead to a reserve reduction and so that the insurer has adequate time to actually reduce the reserves, if appropriate.

In addition, the date is important because the recorded values of claims on this date often are used in dividend, retro, and deductible premium calculations.

## A Typical Claims Review

Some accounts may simply review the loss runs they receive and then call the claims adjuster with questions or comments. At a minimum, it is important to be sure that:

- all claims included on the loss run actually belong to the company;
- claims that are closed are accurately reflected as such; and
- large reserves or changes in reserves seem reasonable.

As hard as it may be to believe, it is not all that unusual for a claim to be assigned to the wrong company. In addition, this type of paper review educates managers about the financial impact that a worker's injuries may have on a company.

If reserves—or claim payments—seem unreasonable, the business owner or agent should check with the adjuster. The adjuster should be able and willing to explain the rationale for the size of the reserve. It is important to remember that carriers retain the right to make final decisions on claims, especially in guaranteed cost and dividend programs. However, even when these types of plans are used, insurers often will listen to reasonable arguments for adjusting the reserve amount. The insured also may be aware of important details that affect the claim.

In many situations, especially when there is a high frequency of claims, adjusters will meet face-to-face with insureds to conduct *claim reviews*. Cases are discussed individually, with the insured providing ideas and information on the cases. Often, arrangements can be made to return an injured employee to light-duty work during these reviews.

A general premise of insurance is that, once a claim is filed with the insurance company, the insurer has the final say in how the claim is handled. Courts have upheld this right in cases where only the insurance company's money is at risk. However, many courts have held that the situation is different in cases where insureds are retrospectively responsible for claim payments made by the insurance company.

One frequently cited case is *Transport Indemnity Company v. Dahlen Transport, Inc.,* 161 N.W.2d 546 (Minn. 1968). In *Transport,* the Minnesota Supreme Court ruled that the insurer can be required to produce evidence that settlements were made in good faith and were not an effort to escape from its responsibility under excess coverage provisions. This and more recent cases have reasoned that insurance companies may face conflicts of interest in adjusting claims under retrospectively rated policies. Often, spending the insured's money to settle a claim quickly could ultimately save the insurance company money.

These types of cases reinforce the value of claim reviews and support the idea that the insured's vested interest should be considered in good faith claim settlement procedures.

## Location Coding

Claims location coding often helps both the insured and insurer zero in on problem areas. Claims may be coded by location for businesses with multiple sites or departments so that loss data is tied to specific areas of the company. Loss control and safety management can then be targeted to areas with high frequency or severity of claims.

A sample location coding system for a fictitious bank follows:

| | Sample Location Coding System |
| --- | --- |

**Numeric Coding Using Internal Department Codes**
**Seven-Digit Field**

| Claim Code | Location/Department | Claim Code | Location/Department |
| --- | --- | --- | --- |
| | | 0300000 | Bank #2, Division #3 |
| 0100000 | Bank Holding Company, Division #01 | 0350000 | Crawford Branch Office, Dept. #50 |
| 0101000 | Executive Department, Dept. #01 | 0350001 | Lobby Area |
| 0102000 | Audit Department, Dept. #02 | 0350002 | Teller Area |
| 0103000 | Facilities Maintenance, Dept. #03 | 0350003 | Outside Pedestrian Areas |
| 0104000 | Risk Management Department, Dept. #04 | 0350004 | Outside Parking Areas |
| 0105000 | Commercial Loan Department, Dept. #05 | | |
| 0106000 | Trust Department, Dept. #06 | 0352000 | Simmons Branch Office,   Dept. #52 |
| | | 0352001 | Lobby Area |
| | | 0352002 | Teller Area |
| 0200000 | Bank #1, Division #02 | 0352003 | Outside Pedestrian Areas |
| | | 0352004 | Outside Parking Areas |
| 0210000 | Main St. Branch Office, Dept. #10 | | |
| 0210001 | Lobby Area | 0354000 | Clyde Branch Office, Dept. #54 |
| 0210002 | Teller Area | 0354001 | Lobby Area |
| 0210003 | Outside Pedestrian Areas | 0354002 | Teller Area |
| 0210004 | Outside Parking Areas | 0354003 | Outside Pedestrian Areas |
| | | 0354004 | Outside Parking Areas |
| 0212000 | Third Ave. Branch Office, Dept. #12 | | |
| 0212001 | Lobby Area | 0360000 | Residential Loan Department, Dept. #60 |
| 0212002 | Teller Area | 0362000 | Maintenance, Dept. #62 |
| 0212003 | Outside Pedestrian Areas | | |
| 0212004 | Outside Parking Areas | 0380000 | Free-standing ATM's, Dept. 80 |
| | | 0380025 | Main St. ATM, Loc. #025 |
| 0214000 | South Twp. Branch Office, Dept. #14 | 0380026 | Clifford St. ATM, Loc. #026 |
| 0214001 | Lobby Area | 0380027 | Simon Ave. ATM, Loc. #027 |
| 0214002 | Teller Area | 0380028 | Fourth Ave. ATM, Loc. #028 |
| 0214003 | Outside Pedestrian Areas | 0380029 | West End ATM, Loc. #029 |
| 0214004 | Outside Parking Areas | 0380030 | Northside ATM, Loc. #030 |
| | | 0380031 | Tenth St. ATM, Loc. #031 |
| 0216000 | Chelsea Branch Office, Dept. #16 | 0380032 | Dilson Market ATM, Loc. #032 |
| 0216001 | Lobby Area | 0380033 | Craig St. ATM, Loc. #033 |
| 0216002 | Teller Area | 0380034 | Crussman ATM, Loc. #034 |
| 0216003 | Outside Pedestrian Areas | | |
| 0216004 | Outside Parking Areas | | |
| | | **Key:** | |
| 0270000 | Free-standing ATM's, Dept. #70 | First 2 digits = Internal Accounting Division | |
| 0270020 | Bridgetown ATM,  Loc. #020 | Second set of 3 digits = Department | |
| 0270021 | Carlos ATM, Loc. #021 | Last 2 digits = Location | |
| 0270022 | Chase ATM, Loc. #022 | | |
| 0270023 | Stager ATM, Loc. #023 | | |

The chart illustrates location coding for a holding company with two subsidiary banks. The first two digits of each code represent the division number, the next two digits represent the department code, and the last three digits represent locations within the department. All individuals who report claims should be trained in using them so the codes are indicated on initial claim reports.

## Return to Work Programs

Return to work programs (RTW)—which also are called modified work or light-duty—are designed to return employees to the job as soon as possible—even with physical restrictions. For example, an assembly line worker may be able to do her normal job with the exception of lifting items weighing more than ten pounds. A light-duty program would modify her job so that another worker lifted heavier items for her, or she could be placed in a line where lifting is not required.

When returning employees to modified work, employers need to exercise care that the job truly falls within the confines of any physical restrictions placed on the employee by the treating physician. One way to do this is to write specific job descriptions for each position—regular and light-duty—so that physicians have a clearer picture of the physical demands. Another way is to videotape individuals doing specific jobs and to submit the tapes to the physician so she can better determine whether the restricted employee can do the job. Some businesses allocate a few desk jobs as light-duty positions so they are available if needed.

RTW programs are important because injured workers are more likely to successfully return to regular employment if they are not off for extensive periods of time. They continue to contribute to the company. This is especially important when experienced, skilled employees are injured. Employers need to monitor the physical restrictions, however, so that employees can be moved progressively through various work-hardening positions.

RTW programs can be creatively developed. For example, an experienced employee of a bank underwent surgery for work-related carpal tunnel syndrome in both wrists. She held a job that required working on a computer, and no other employee was as well qualified to do her job. The bank hired a temporary worker to do any typing that was necessary, and the injured employee dictated what the temp should enter. This not only got her work done but also highlighted her value to her.

### ADA Implications

The workers compensation system is not directly linked to the Americans with Disabilities Act (ADA). However, the ADA does have implications for injured workers.

The ADA prohibits discrimination against a "qualified individual with a disability" *because of* the disability. A "qualified individual" is an individual with a disability who can perform the essential functions of a job with or without "reasonable accommodation." In other words, employers must make reasonable accommodations to allow a qualified worker who is disabled to do a job. Reasonable accommodation is not defined in the law, but it is not supposed to impose an undue hardship on the employer. The law defines disability as a physical *or mental* impairment that substantially limits one or more of the *major life activities* of the individual, a record of such an impairment, or being regarded as having the impairment.

Prior to the ADA, some employers were not interested in bringing workers who had been injured on the job back to work if they were disabled. The ADA potentially changes that. If an injured worker is considered to have a disability for purposes of the ADA, the employer must permit her return or face possible legal action. Even though the workers compensation laws do not encompass injury caused by discrimination, they do not shield employers from possible ADA action. Thus, if an employee has a permanent back injury "that substantially limits one or more of the major life activities," failure to provide employment to an otherwise qualified worker could lead to problems.

The ADA applies to employers engaged in an industry affecting commerce with fifteen or more employees for twenty weeks or more, so small companies may not be impacted by it.

## Integrated Disability Management

Integrated disability management (IDM) is a system that integrates the management of workers compensation-related disabilities with nonoccupational disability management. The theory is that the individual is looked at as a whole, and occupational disabilities are not segregated from nonoccupational disabilities. There has been success in this approach to managing employee disabilities, especially among self-insurers. However, since workers compensation is a state-regulated system, and nonoccupational benefits are regulated under ERISA, integrating the programs does pose problems.

## Loss Prevention Incentive Programs

Some companies believe that incentive programs designed around accident-free work days can lead to a safer workplace. Others believe the idea may just encourage workers not to report injuries instead of actually making people work more safely.

When a safety incentive program is desired, it can be structured in a number of ways. It usually awards employees with gifts as safety improvements are made or accident history improves. There usually is a large award if a department meets a certain goal in preventing accidents over a period of a year.

For example, a manufacturer's modification is 1.60 because of poor loss history. This means that the company is paying 60 percent more for workers compensation coverage than an average competitor. The company implements a safety incentive program to encourage managers and employees to avoid accidents. The plan could be structured with individual departments grouped into safety teams. Each team member may be given a small award, such as a lunch certificate, for each month in which there are no lost time accidents and a larger certificate if there are no accidents. For each accident-free quarter worked, larger awards are presented. Teams that work an entire year without an accident may receive cash awards. The same program could be designed so that a specific percentage improvement in safety earns recognition.

Regardless of the specifics of such programs, they do highlight senior management's commitment to safety, which is the key to safety improvement over time.

## Premium Allocation Systems

There are many ways that workers compensation premiums, including the variable cost of claims, can be allocated across operating units. An allocation system is valuable in claims management when it charges individual operating units for their own claims. It can be used as part of the unit managers' annual performance reviews, which is an excellent way to encourage managers to pay attention to workers compensation claims. Safety and claims management thus become ingrained into their jobs.

In a guaranteed cost insurance program, the simplest allocation systems assign the premium as a percentage of each unit's payroll. No unit safety or claims management incentive is built into this type of system; allocations are not sensitive to claims. Losses should play a part in the allocation if it is to provide a claims management incentive.

At the beginning of a fiscal year, a portion of the insurance premium may be allocated as a percentage of payroll. Then, the unit may be charged for a percentage of each claim's incurred value. Once again, this presents a financial incentive for good experience and a penalty for poor experience. It also helps to build safety into the culture of the company.

## Financial Impact

The value of effectively managing a workers compensation program cannot be underestimated. The idea of creating a safer workplace should be the defining goal of all employers. The workers compensation system provides financial incentives to do just that—through experience and schedule rating and optional financial plans.

What should never be overlooked, however, are the hidden costs of employee injuries—the cost of finding and training replacement workers, the cost of losing experienced employees to injury, and the cost of lowered morale after a serious workplace accident. Cost-management programs can heighten awareness of the vital importance—to both management and labor—of preventing and managing employee injuries.

# Chapter 13

# Issues in Workers Compensation

## Introduction

Several issues have found their way into the courtroom for decisions on whether injuries fall within the workers compensation system or not. Is workers compensation the exclusive remedy for injured workers? Who is to provide coverage for leased workers? What does "in the course of employment" mean? Are mental injuries suffered by employees compensable?

This chapter focuses on such issues. The discussions do not exhaust the subject matter, but they do present a solid base of information for those who work within the workers compensation system.

## Exclusive Remedy

The workers compensation system stood for more than fifty years as the sole recourse of employees injured on the job. This *exclusive remedy* provided injured employees with scheduled medical and lost-wage benefits in exchange for their giving up the right to sue the employer. The statutes provided immunity to employers from common law actions brought by employees seeking payment for injuries arising out of and in the course of employment. However, since the case of *Duprey v. Shane,* 249 P.2d 8 (Cal. 1952), (a workers compensation and medical malpractice case in which the employee injured in the course of employment was also treated by her employer, a doctor, and who was allowed to circumvent the workers compensation exclusive remedy based on negligence) various legal doctrines have eroded the exclusive remedy concept and the seemingly clear-cut insurance situation. For example, common law suits against employers have been successfully brought on the basis of dual capacity, intentional tort, and third-party-over doctrines.

## Dual Capacity

The *dual capacity* doctrine holds that an employer normally shielded by the exclusive remedy rule may be liable for additional damages for committing a wrongful act that is not related to the role of employer. This occurs when the employer is judged to occupy a second capacity in which the exposure is common to the public in general.

A classic illustration of a potential dual capacity situation is that of a soda-bottler's delivery man injured by an exploding bottle during the stocking of a merchant's shelves. The soda-bottler employer is responsible for workers compensation for its employee, the delivery man. He also could be held responsible as the manufacturer of the bottle if the injured delivery man, as a member of the general public, decided to pursue a products liability action against the manufacturer. The decisive test of this doctrine, then, is not how separate or different the second capacity of the employer is from the first. It is concerned with whether the second capacity of manufacturer generates obligations unrelated to those flowing from the first, that of an employer.

Currently, courts in a majority of states generally reject the dual capacity doctrine. See, for example, *State v. Purdy*, 601 P.2d 258 (Alas. 1979) and *Billy v. Consolidated Machine Tool Corp.*, 412 N.E.2d 934 (N.Y. 1980). Furthermore, some state legislatures have forbidden or limited the possibility of dual capacity lawsuits through statutory law.

In order to clearly address dual capacity lawsuits, both the workers compensation form and the general liability form were revised. The part two section of the workers compensation policy—employers liability insurance—specifcally provides that damages claimed against the insured in a capacity other than as an employer may be paid. The current commercial general liability form specifically excludes bodily injury to an employee whether the insured is liable as an employer or in any other capacity. Thus these two forms make it as clear as possible that injury to an employee is to be handled under the workers compensation and employers liability policy regardless of whether dual capacity is claimed or not.

## Intentional Tort

In many jurisdictions, injuries caused by an employer's intentional actions have been ruled not to arise out of the course of employment.

Furthermore, public policy does not permit an employer immunity from civil actions when the employer intended to injure or otherwise harm an employee. Regardless of whether the employer's *acts* or the *results* of his acts were intended, many courts have decided that workers compensation is simply not the sole remedy in such situations. Some examples of this rationale are illustrated below.

The issue before an Illinois appellate court was whether exclusive remedy bars a suit against the employer of a pizza delivery man when the employer knew with substantial certainty that the delivery man would be attacked while making a delivery. That court decided to allow such suits if it can be shown that the employer had a specific intent to injure or cause injury to the employee. The claimants could not show that intent, so the case was dismissed. However, the point was made that the exclusive remedy of the workers compensation system could be bypassed under certain conditions. The case is *Bercaw v. Domino's Pizza, Inc.*, 630 N.E.2d 166 (Ill. App. Ct. 1994).

In *Fricke v. Owens-Corning Fiberglass Corp.*, 571 So.2d 130 (La. 1990), a Louisiana court indicated that it is not necessary for the employer to intend to inflict actual damage or that actions be malicious. Intending to inflict either a harmful or offensive contact without the employee's consent was enough to constitute intent.

In *Pursell v. Pizza Inn, Inc.* 786 P.2d 716 (Okla. Ct. App. 1990), employees alleged that their supervisors deliberately sexually battered and harassed them at work. After hearing the case, the court decided that such allegations of willful, intentional, or even violent conduct by the employer took the case out of the exclusive domain of workers compensation.

In *Gulden v. Crown Zellerbach Corp.*, 890 F.2d 195 (9th Cir. 1989), employees who had been ordered to clean up a PCB spill without protective clothing claimed the employer intended to injure them. An Oregon court of appeals decided that a jury could conclude that the intention to injure was deliberate where the employer had an opportunity to weigh the consequences and choose among courses of action. Therefore, allegations of intentional injury could not be dismissed by summary judgment on the basis of the state's workers compensation law. The employees sued based on tort liability. Similarly, in *Richie v. Rogers Cartage Co.*, 626 N.E.2d 1012 (Ohio Ct. App. 1994), an Ohio appeals court decided that a lawsuit by an employee against an employer could not be summarily dismissed if the question of company intent existed. The court said that there had to be a trial to determine whether the employer committed an intentional wrong.

The intentional tort exception to the exclusive remedy doctrine is not universally accepted in all jurisdictions, and the debate will continue. Court decisions will vary from one jurisdiction to another, and employers should be aware of decisions not only in the area where their company is domiciled but in all areas where they conduct business activities. Responsible employers also should realize that many states' workers compensation laws provide the right to bring tort action against an employer for injuries resulting from the employer's willful, deliberate conduct.

## Third-Party-Over

The *third-party-over* doctrine involves the injured employee suing a third party, who subsequently is able to bring an action against the employer. For example, the employer may have contractually assumed the obligations and liabilities of the third party. For example, Coastal Manufacturing Co. hires M&J Maintenance Co. to do maintenance work. M&J agrees to hold Coastal harmless and to indemnify it for injury to M&J workers. An M&J employee is injured when an overhead crane runs into his scaffolding. The employee files for workers compensation benefits from M&J. In addition, he sues Coastal for negligence in operating the crane. Coastal turns the lawsuit over to M&J because the maintenance company had agreed to indemnify Coastal. M&J ends up paying workers compensation benefits, defending the lawsuit, and paying the lawsuit settlement.

The employers liability section of the policy specifically pays for damages for which the insured is liable to a third party by reason of a claim or suit by that third party. The commercial general liability forms specifically apply the workers compensation exclusion to any obligation to share damages with or repay someone else who must pay damages. However, this exclusion does not apply to liability assumed by the insured under an insured contract. Using the example of Coastal and M&J, M&J's general liability form will defend and pay if necessary because of the exception to the exclusion. M&J's employers liability insurance (part two on the workers compensation policy) will not apply since liability assumed under a contract is not covered.

## Other Possible Doctrines

It is safe to say that the exclusive remedy rule of workers compensation will continue to be the subject of repeated assaults. The following discussion is not the final word on this issue, but it does offer some examples of arguments being made.

In *Kerans v. Porter Paint Co.*, 575 N.E.2d 428 (Ohio 1991), the claimant alleged that she was sexually molested on five separate occasions by a coworker and that Porter Paint did nothing to discipline or reprimand the coworker. Kerans sued based on sexual harassment. Porter Paint made a motion for judgment without trial based on the exclusive remedy of workers compensation. The Ohio trial court granted the company's motion, but on appeal, the Supreme Court stated that the workers compensation statute did not provide the exclusive remedy for claims based on sexual harassment. The Court decided that workers compensation provides coverage for economic losses resulting from accidents. Sexual harassment did not usually result in economic loss, but in loss of dignity and self-esteem. Therefore, workers compensation was not the remedy for the damages suffered by the claimant.

Another example is *Bunger v. Lawson Co.*, 696 N.E.2d 1029 (Ohio 1998). Bunger was working late and was robbed. She claimed psychological injury and post-traumatic stress and sought workers compensation benefits. The state industrial commission said no. When the issue went to trial, a lower court declared that she was not entitled to workers compensation benefits because she had not suffered physical injury. In addition, she had no right to sue because the condition arose during the scope of employment. The Ohio Supreme Court reversed this finding and declared that "Workers compensation does not foreclose an employee who has suffered purely psychological injuries from pursuing a common law remedy". The court reasoned that psychological injuries were not included within the definition of *injury* in the state workers compensation law. Therefore, such injuries could not be included in any grant of employer immunity from a lawsuit for any *injury* suffered by an employee.

Another example is *Errand v. Cascade Steel Rolling Mills, Inc.*, 888 P.2d 544 (Ore. 1995). In this case, the Oregon Supreme Court allowed a lawsuit against an employer by an employee to proceed as an exception to the exclusivity rule of the workers compensation system. The court decided that the state law made workers compensation the exclusive remedy for "compensable injuries," and that where an employee's injuries have been determined not to fit into that category, the exclusivity status of workers compensation does not apply.

In *Kerans*, the Court equated bodily injury with economic loss and declared that sexual harassment resulted in more than mere economic loss; therefore, workers compensation was not the exclusive remedy. In *Bunger*, the court said that psychological injury was not bodily injury as defined by law; therefore, the workers compensation system was not the proper forum to seek compensation. In *Errand*, the injuries suffered by the employee did not fit into the definition of compensable injuries under the state workers compensation law. These cases illustrate that "bodily injury" is subject to court interpretation. If alleged damages are deemed to either not include bodily injury or extend beyond the legal meaning of that term, a court may rule that workers compensation is not the claimant's sole path of recovery.

Exclusive remedy might also be breached when the claimant denies that the injury occurred *in the course of employment*. If the claimant was injured outside the course of employment, there is no causal connection between the injury and employment. A tort claim, then, based on negligence against the employer may be applicable. Some examples of this are *Middlekauff v. Allstate Insurance Co.*, 439 S.E.2d 394 (Va. 1994); *Williams v. Martin Marietta Energy Systems, Inc.*, 651 N.E.2d 55 (Ohio Ct. App. 1994); and *Copeland v. Boots Pharmaceuticals*, 916 P.2d 277 (Okla. Ct. App. 1996).

Uninsured motorists (UM) benefits can also be used as an avenue of attack against the exclusivity rule of the workers compensation system. In *Conzo v. Aetna Insurance Co.*, 705 A.2d 1020 (Ct. 1998), the issue was whether an employee injured in the course of employment while occupying the employer's car is entitled to collect UM benefits from the employer. The employee had already collected workers compensation benefits and then sought UM benefits. The state supreme court allowed the employee to collect from both sources. Note that this is a minority position at this time.

Finally, another erosion in the exclusive remedy doctrine involves the preempting of state workers compensation laws by federal laws. The theory used is that the employer, through its actions or inaction, has violated a federal law, and the injured employee has a right to sue for any damages suffered based on that federal law. For example, migrant farm workers, injured while riding in their employer's van, received workers compensation benefits under Florida law and then sued in federal court. They argued that their injuries were caused in part by the employer's violation of motor vehicle safety provisions of the Migrant and Seasonal Agricultural Worker Protection Act. The employer claimed workers compensation as the exclusive remedy. The case went all the way to the United States Supreme Court. The case, *Adams Fruit Co., Inc., v. Barrett*, 494 U.S.638 (1990), ended when the Supreme Court affirmed that the federal migrant protection act does preempt state law. Therefore, workers compensation is not the sole remedy.

Note that Congress moved to overrule this decision by amending the federal law. However, federal laws can be used to ignore the exclusive remedy idea behind workers compensation. Other examples of federal laws that should be considered are the Employment Retirement Income Security Act (ERISA), the Americans With Disabilities Act (ADA), and the Family and Medical Leave Act (FMLA).

## Mental Stress Claims

Coverage under workers compensation insurance applies to bodily injury *by accident* and bodily injury *by disease*(including resulting death). The agreement does contain two stipulations: 1) bodily injury by accident must occur during the policy period; and 2) bodily injury by disease must be caused or aggravated by conditions of employment, with the employee's last exposure to those conditions occurring during the policy period.

The workers compensation policy does not define bodily injury. This can, and often does, lead to disputes over the question of coverage for mental stress claims. Is mental stress compensable under the law?

Generally, workers compensation cases involving emotional or mental conditions can be divided into three groups:

1) Mental stimulus resulting in physical injury
2) Physical trauma resulting in mental injury
3) Mental stimulus resulting in mental injury

Most jurisdictions and workers compensation boards have no problem awarding benefits under the first two groupings because the employee is disabled by an injury that is associated with a physical manifestation. In cases of mental injury as a result of mental stress, decisions vary from jurisdiction to jurisdiction. For example, courts in Illinois, Mississippi, and Texas have decided mental injury caused by mental stress is a compensable injury. Courts in Kansas, Wyoming, Ohio, and Wisconsin have denied workers compensation benefits for such injuries.

The most substantial factor found in those cases denying compensation without bodily injury is the difficulty of proving injury. Because mental injury is vague, shadowy, intangible, and could be within the control of the sufferer, it was feared that the disability could too easily be simulated. It is as if the courts were saying they could not comprehend a method to objectively value a claim based on mental pain without any accompanying physical injury to evaluate. Therefore, such claims had to be denied.

Jurisdictions that permit compensation for mental injury claims without accompanying bodily injury emphasize that the difficulty of formulating appropriate legal tests does not justify denying the claims. For example, in *NPS Corp. v. Insurance Co. of North America*, 517 A.2d 1211 (N.J. Super. Ct. App. Div. 1986), the New Jersey appeals court held that emotional distress and mental anguish caused to an employee by sexual harassment from a fellow employee constituted bodily injury. The court stated that New Jersey has come to recognize that mental and emotional distress is just as real as physical pain and that its valuation is no more difficult. Within that framework, the court disagreed with the defendant's argument that bodily injury necessarily entails some physical or corporeal harm caused by the application of external violence. The court said, "We are unable to separate a person's nerves and tensions from his body since, clearly, emotional trauma can be as disabling to the body as a visible physical wound".

The dispute over whether bodily injury must be present in order to recover for a mental injury claim will not be settled soon. At this time, a majority of authorities hold that bodily injury does not include mental stress. If there is a discernible trend, it is toward recognition of mental injury due to stress and tension. The reasoning: mental injury may be brought about in the same manner as stress causes a heart attack or other physical condition.

There is another aspect to consider. Since the workers compensation policy applies to injury *by accident*, can mental stress be equated with *accident* for recovery under the policy? Mental stress severe enough to cause disability generally does not develop overnight. If it is a gradual process over a long period, can it be termed an accident? The workers compensation policy does not define the word. However *Black's Law Dictionary* does offer the following: with reference to workers compensation acts, an act is an event that takes place without one's foresight or expectation; an undesigned, sudden, and unexpected event.

Many insurance terms are subject to differing judicial interpretations, "accident" is no exception. The general principle is that impairments, even physical ones, developing in imperceptible stages as a result of particular work over an appreciable period of time are not compensable as accidental injuries. This principle has been adhered to in cases that decline compensation for a mental disability claim. For example, in *Lawson v. Employers Insurance of Wausau*, 330 F.Supp. 321 (E.D. Tenn. 1971), a federal court decided that a general mental breakdown resulting from overwork or long employment at a particular type of activity was not a compensable accident. The court stated that the employee's anxiety and hypertension did not disable the employee within the meaning of the state workers compensation law.

Other jurisdictions have ignored the general principle upheld in *Lawson* and granted compensation, equating a gradual deterioration of mental stability with an accident. The Supreme Court of Arizona in *Fireman's Fund Insurance Co. v. Industrial Commission*, 579 P.2d 555 (Ariz. 1978) held that an employee who suffered a mental breakdown as a result of constant work pressures did sustain a personal injury claim arising out of and in the course of her employment. The court agreed that the mental breakdown resulted from a gradual buildup of stress and tension at work and was sufficiently unanticipated to be called unexpected. It therefore was accidental within the meaning of the statute providing compensation.

The differing court decisions on compensation for impairments that develop over a period of time are reduced to disagreeing about whether accident means only a sudden, one-shot trauma or whether the word can encompass gradual trauma.

## In the Course of Employment

In order for workers compensation benefits to apply, bodily injury to an employee must arise *out of and in the course of employment*. Aside from the issue of just what bodily injury includes, another point of contention can be just what "out of and in the course of employment" means. Since neither the various states' laws nor the policy define this phrase and the workers compensation policy itself does not offer a definition, the courts have taken on the task.

"The test of the right to participate in the workers compensation fund is ... whether a causal connection existed between an employee's injury and his employment either through the activities, the conditions, or the environment of the employment". This is a quote from an Ohio state supreme court decision, *Bralle v. Daugherty*, 401 N.E.2d 302 (Ohio 1980). It points out that an employee must be injured as a result of employment before workers compensation or employers liability insurance will kick in; that is, the employment has to cause the injury. If a causal connection between the injury and the employment is disputed, such disputes are decided on a case-by-case basis. Following are some examples.

In *Appeal of Griffin*, 671 A.2d 541 (N.E. 1996), Griffin was injured in a fight with coworkers and filed for benefits. The compensation board decided his injuries did not arise out of and in the course of employment, so Griffin appealed to the court. The New Hampshire appeals court stated that the injury did arise out of employment. The court found that Griffin was driving his coworkers back from a meal and that the fight started with a quarrel about his driving. The driving was work-related and the fight was about the driving; thus, the injuries were work-related.

In *Williams v. Martin Marietta Energy Systems, Inc.*, 651 N.E.2d 55 (Ohio Ct. App. 1994), an Ohio appeals court decided that an injury suffered by an employee during a blood drive did not arise out of and in the course of employment. The employer had no control over the attempted drawing of blood from Williams. The employee's participation in the blood drive was not a regular incident and condition of employment and so the injuries suffered by the employee were not compensable.

In *Copeland v. Boots Pharmaceuticals,* 916 P.2d 277 (Okla. Ct. App. 1996), Copeland was a traveling sales rep. While on sales calls, she stopped for the night in a hotel. Copeland was bitten by a spider in the hotel and filed for workers compensation benefits. After benefits were denied, Copeland appealed. The appeals court in Oklahoma decided her injuries did not arise from her employment. The court said that the injuries did not stem from an employment-related risk. There was no connection between her job and the risk of encountering spiders; it was a personal risk and not a business risk.

## Relationship to Employment

There are some activities engaged in by employees that raise the question whether such activities are related to employment. Examples are recreational activities (such as the company softball team or picnic), coming and going, horseplay and fights, and alcohol or drug consumption.

Many employers sponsor picnics or sporting events where employees may get hurt. If such activities are paid for and supervised by the employer for the purpose of generating or improving the employer-employee relationship, an injury sustained by an employee can be considered to be in the course of employment.

In general, injuries sustained by an employee while coming to and going from work are not considered employment-related. There are exceptions to this rule, which usually apply when the employee is doing some work-related activity during the travel or if the employer controls the site where the injury occurred, such as a company parking lot.

As for injury during horseplay or fights, the circumstances dictate whether the injury is sustained in the course of employment. If an employee is on the job and gets hurt because of the horseplay of another person, that injury is usually compensable. On the other hand, if the employee perpetrating the horseplay gets hurt, that usually is not considered work-related. The situation is similar when it comes to a fight. The instigator of the fight usually is not entitled to workers compensation benefits, but the injured victim can be depending on the circumstances. If the fight is personal (for example, a political disagreement), the injury cannot be said to occur in the course of employment. If the fight is business related (for example, an argument over possession of a tool), the injury may be considered in the course of employment and be compensable.

Finally, standing alone, alcohol or drug consumption is not usually sufficient to defeat recovery of workers compensation benefits if the user is injured at work. If the worker is rendered incapable of doing his or her job due to alcohol or drug intake and is injured while under the influence, that injury is not generally considered to have occurred in the course of employment. The employee, in effect, abandoned the job through voluntary action and the injury is not considered to be in the course of employment. On the other hand, if the employee has consumed alcohol or drugs but can still function on the job and is injured, for example, at his station, that injury is in the course of employment and workers compensation benefits apply. Some states may have legislated differently in regard to alcohol or drug consumption and compensability.

To summarize, even though the workers compensation system is not based on fault or negligence, there are conditions governing when benefits are to be paid. Just because a person is an employee and gets hurt, does not guarantee workers compensation benefits.

## Employment of Minors

State employment laws govern minors. The scope of coverage under workers compensation and employers liability insurance for minors employed contrary to law varies by state. Therefore, it is not practical to apply general statements to particular cases.

When a *legally* employed minor is injured in the course of employment, the workers compensation system functions the same as in any employee injury situation. That is, the injured minor is eligible for all benefits prescribed by the state's workers compensation law, to be paid by the employer's workers compensation insurance. However, when *illegally* employed minors are injured in the course of employment, employers may find themselves in difficult situations regarding insurance coverage, particularly when the employer has knowingly permitted the illegal employment.

Note that a provision of the workers compensation policy makes clear that the insured is responsible for any payments *in excess of regular workers compensation benefits,* including penalties imposed because of injury to any person knowingly employed in violation of the law. Therefore, if an employer allows a minor to work in a situation that the law limits to adult workers, and the minor is injured, the employer will pay any penalties imposed upon him or her by the state. The workers compensation insurer will pay only the standard benefits. Some states impose a 50 percent increase in benefits (including Arizona, California, and Missouri). Illinois requires a 50 percent increase for minors under sixteen. Other states require *double* compensation (or 200 percent), as in Alabama and Ohio. In Arkansas, double compensation is required unless the minor misrepresented his age in writing to the employer. Mississippi and New Jersey mandate double compensation except for students fourteen and over who are employed between semesters or who are involved in on-the-job training. Rhode Island requires a tripling (300 percent) of benefits. In Wisconsin, double compensation is mandated for minors employed without a permit, and triple compensation is required when minors are employed in prohibited work.

The employers liability section of the policy excludes coverage of bodily injury to an employee hired in violation of the law if the employer or his executive officers actually know of the violation. The employers liability section also excludes punitive or exemplary damages because of bodily injury to an employee employed in violation of law. So, if the injured minor is allowed to sue the employer for personal injuries in lieu of seeking workers compensation benefits, any punitive damages will be paid by the employer and not the workers compensation insurer.

In a small number of states, including Oklahoma and Vermont, statutory workers compensation benefits are not extended to illegally employed minors. However, the employer is not relieved of financial responsibility. On the contrary, the minor is allowed to sue the employer at common law and the workers compensation policy need not respond. Common law actions may also be initiated against an employer by the parents of an illegally employed injured minor.

New Jersey and Illinois, for example, extend benefits to illegally employed minors by statute, but also give the injured minor the option of statutory benefits or suing the employer at common law. The employers liability section (part two) of the workers compensation and employers liability policy applies to liability of the employer under such circumstances. This is subject to two important exceptions: 1) punitive or exemplary damages because of bodily injury to an employee hired in violation of law; and 2) bodily injury to an employee while employed in violation of law with the "actual knowledge" of the employer or an executive officer.

It is important to note, however, that this second exclusion has been held unenforceable in at least one jurisdiction. In *National Grange Mutual Insurance Co. v. Schneider*, 392 A.2d 641 (N.J. Super. Ct. Law Div. 1978), the insurer relied on this exclusion in denying employers liability coverage to a meat market where a thirteen-year-old (hired knowingly without a work certificate even though he was too young to obtain one) severely injured an arm in a meat grinder. The claim was entered under the employers liability part of the policy because the minor had exercised the option given to illegally employed minors in New Jersey to sidestep the workers compensation's exclusive remedy provisions and bring suit at common law. Because the damages would have been covered had the minor brought claim under the workers compensation part of the policy, the court held it was against public policy for the insurer to be allowed to exclude coverage under the employers liability insurance. "The reformers who created workers compensation and factory law remedies for injured employees and industrially abused minors simply would not purposely deprive an illegally employed thirteen-year-old, who claims injury by the negligence of his employer, insurance protection granted routinely to almost everyone else . . . If the insurers hesitate to cover illegal employments, perhaps their remedy is reimbursement from the employer and not deprivation of the employee. The exclusion may not be applied to an illegally employed minor without violating New Jersey law."

The New Jersey superior court again considered the issue and arrived at the same conclusion in *Variety Farms, Inc. v. New Jersey Manufacturers Insurance Co.*, 410 A.2d 696 (N.J. Super. Ct. App. Div. 1980). Here, a fifteen-year-old lost an arm when allowed to operate power-driven equipment in spite of the state's labor law restricting anyone under sixteen from such work. As in *Grange*, the minor exercised his option to bring suit at common law rather than accept the statutory benefits. The insurer denied coverage based on the employers liability exclusion pertaining to employees employed in violation of the law with the knowledge of the insured. However, the court held that the exclusion could not apply. The exclusion "would be so repugnant to the letter and spirit of the state workers compensation law and so contrary to public policy as to be unenforceable in a case such as the one here involved."

# Principals and Contractors

The workers compensation laws of a majority of states impose liability on principals for compensation benefits to employees of contractors or subcontractors. These statutes vary from state to state but usually are qualified by a provision imposing liability on the owner (principal) *only* in the absence of workers compensation insurance provided by the subcontractor. For example, the statute of Wisconsin reads: "An employer shall be liable for compensation to an employee of a contractor or subcontractor who is not subject to this chapter, or who has not complied with the conditions of the statute in any case where such employer would have been liable for compensation if such employee had been working directly for him."

The status of the injured worker as an independent contractor or an employee is imputed. The Internal Revenue Service (IRS) has a checklist to determine the status of a worker for income tax purposes. Some of the items included are:

- who delivers instructions and who complies with them;
- how is training done;
- where does direction and control come from;
- who does the hiring, supervising, and paying;
- who sets the hours of work;
- who has the right to discharge a worker and terminate the work;
- who furnishes the tools and materials; and
- who has supplied the investment or capital?

The main consideration noted in this IRS list is the idea of control. Who controls the situation, and what is the relationship between the one who exercises control and the one injured? That idea of control is also behind the decisions of some courts when it comes to the status of injured persons. In *Claim of Griffin*, 466 N.W.2d 148 (N.D. 1991), the supreme court in North Dakota stated that "in determining whether a person is an employee or an independent contractor, the primary test is the right to control. Under that test, if the person for whom the work is being done has the right of control, whether he exercises it or not, and is concerned not only with the result of the work but also with the manner and method of its doing, he is held to be an employer and the person doing the work is his employee. On the other hand, if he is concerned merely with the result of the work and has no control over the details of its doing, the person doing the work is held to be an independent contractor."

In general, a principal or contractor is not held responsible for the workers compensation claims of employees of contractors or subcontractors unless the subordinate employer has failed to provide coverage. This can happen, for example, through the expiration of a subcontractor's workers compensation insurance, the failure of a subcontractor to provide proper coverage, or because a subcontractor has too few employees to fall under the workers compensation statutes. There are, however, exceptions to this. By statute in several jurisdictions the principal may be liable: 1) if the work contracted is his usual business or occupation; or 2) if he retains control of the premises and supervises the work. In states where a minimum number of employees governs coverage under the act, liability may be passed upward to a contractor or principal who qualifies either because of the number of his own direct employees or because of the combined number involved with several nonqualifying subcontractors. A principal or contractor may also be held liable if the subcontractor's insurance is canceled or the subcontractor's insurer becomes insolvent.

When the principal or contractor is responsible for the compensation due an injured worker, the standard workers compensation and employers liability policy covers the benefits that are due. If the principal or contractor does not carry workers compensation insurance because he has no employees or not enough to require him to comply with the act, this obligation to the employees of subcontractors still applies.

What if the principal is a homeowner who has hired someone to do maintenance work? What if, further, the contractors and subcontractors hired for the job have no workers compensation policies and one of their employees is injured on the job? Typically, the homeowner will not have a workers compensation policy to cover the payment of any required benefits. What does the homeowner do for such coverage?

In general, it is unsafe in any of the states that impose liability on a principal or contractor to permit a contractor or subcontractor to work without workers compensation insurance. A person who fails to check the insurance protection of contractors or subcontractors is gambling for high stakes. This is especially true for homeowners, since homeowners forms do not apply to bodily injury to any person eligible to receive any benefits required to be provided by the insured under any workers compensation law. Therefore, the homeowner cannot rely on the homeowners policy to pay any required benefits.

This leaves few options for the homeowner. He can either self-insure or purchase a workers compensation policy, if possible. The self-insurance option could be expensive especially if the injury is serious or permanent. The purchasing of a workers compensation policy makes more sense financially but could run afoul of state regulations or, more likely, be nearly impossible to purchase in the standard marketplace. The best path for the homeowner would be, as intimated above, to make sure the contractor he hires for repair work carries proper and adequate workers compensation insurance.

In most cases, a principal or contractor that is compelled to pay compensation to an employee of another has an action against the person who is primarily liable. Homeowners should be aware of the fact that they or their insurer can seek recovery from another party if that other party is responsible for the employee's injury.

## Leased Employees

A leased or borrowed employee is defined as one who is dispatched by his employer to another for some service. The leased employee must be loaned with his consent, and he must come under the exclusive control and direction of the employer to whom he is leased. Examples include temporary office workers or workers leased from an employment agency by a contractor to construct a building or drive trucks.

When the leased employee is injured on the job, does workers compensation or general liability insurance apply? If workers compensation applies, is it the exclusive remedy for the injured worker? Whose policy applies, the lessor's or the lessee's? Can the party that provides coverage then seek recovery or pro rata payment from the other involved party?

The fact that the employee is paid by a particular entity is not, in itself, conclusive in determining who is the employer. In general, the party that controls the work is the employer.

When employer A lends an employee to employer B, the latter becomes liable for workers compensation coverage under certain circumstances. For example, a Florida appeals court, in *J.M. Foster, Inc. v. N.A. Logan, Inc.*, 483 So.2d 553 (Fla. Dist. Ct. App. 1986), decided that if the employee has an express or implied contract for hire with employer B, if the work being done is essentially that of employer B, and if the power to control details of the work being done resides in employer B, then employer B is liable for workers compensation benefits.

The three factors noted by the Florida court were also in evidence in a decision by a Louisiana court of appeals. In *Robbins v. Lee*, 505 So.2d 1161

(La. Ct. App. 1987), the court stated that Robbins was not a loaned employee because his act of helping to raise sheet metal was gratuitous and limited in scope and time. There was no contractual relationship and no control over Robbins exercised by Lee.

The United States Tax Court, in *Professional & Executive Leasing, Inc.* 89 TC 225 (1987), established a test consisting of seven factors to determine if an employment relationship exists. The court stated that the following areas had to be examined in order to accurately define the employment relationship: the degree of control over the work of the employees; any significant investment that the leasing company has made in the workplace; the realization of profit or loss by the leasing company; the integration of the work of the leased employees into the regular business operations of the leasing company; the right to hire and terminate; the type of work relationship (i.e., permanent job versus temporary job); how the parties treat the relationship and what the parties consider that relationship to be.

There are contractual and statutory points that need to be considered in addition to legal doctrine.

A firm that leases its employees to another firm may have spelled out in the lease agreement which party must provide the workers compensation coverage. Presuming the existence of such a valid contract, the leased worker has the benefit of knowing coverage exists and all concerned parties are aware of their respective responsibilities.

Obviously, such a contractual agreement would have one of two alternatives. First, one or the other employer will provide workers compensation insurance and employers liability insurance. Second, both employers will provide the necessary coverage.

Under the first scenario, employer A (the lessor) may be required by employer B (the lessee) to provide workers compensation and employers liability insurance. Employer A may add the alternative employer endorsement, WC 00 03 01, to its existing workers compensation policy. This endorsement applies to bodily injury to employees in the course of special or temporary employment by the alternative employer named in the schedule. The insurer agrees, under the terms of WC 00 03 01, to reimburse the alternative employer for the benefits required if the insurer is not permitted to pay the benefits directly to the injured persons.

If both employers agree to provide workers compensation coverage and be liable for the benefits, each should have its own workers compensation policy. The agreement between the two employers may spell out the amounts of benefits and premiums to be paid by the respective parties. It should be noted that the other insurance clause in the workers compensation policy states that benefits and costs covered by the insurance are on a pro rata basis, subject to any limits of liability that may apply.

What if, however, one of the parties reneges on the contract or refuses to sign it? In this case, state laws vary, but, generally, if the lessee employer can't or won't provide workers compensation benefits, that burden will flow back to the lessor employer. One instance of litigation of such statutory employment status is found in *Dockery v. McMillan*, 355 S.E.2d 153 (N.C. Ct. App. 1987). In this case, a North Carolina appeals court held that a general employer is responsible for the payment of compensation benefits because that employer had failed to ascertain whether or not the borrowing employer had workers compensation insurance. The latter employer did not, and the general employer had to pay the benefits.

Any response from the general liability policy to an injured employee has to be considered in light of exclusions (d) and (e) on the commercial general liability coverage form. These are the exclusions dealing with obligations of the insured under workers compensation laws and due to employee injury. The CGL policy of the party deemed to be the employer would exclude coverage for injury to an employee.

It is true that an injured employee, today, is no longer necessarily limited to the exclusive remedy of workers compensation. However, the CGL form is also quite clear in excluding coverage of damages based on dual capacity or third-party-over ideas, ideas that are at the heart of the erosion of the exclusive remedy principle.

What is the result if a leased employee files a claim or a lawsuit against that employer *not* considered to be the employer of record? For example, the employee is leased from employer A to employer B, who becomes legally responsible for workers compensation benefits. The employee is injured while working for employer B; he receives workers compensation benefits from B and then files suit against employer A claiming negligence in the manner of his leasing. The CGL form of employer A responds to such a claim. CGL Exclusion (d) will not apply because the claim does not deal with any obligation arising from a workers compensation law. CGL Exclusion (e) will not apply because the claim is based on the alleged negligence of the insured (employer A) and not his employment of the injured worker. The worker is the employee of employer B.

If employer A then files a third-party-over suit against employer B seeking to share the damages, exclusion (e) (2) (2) of B's CGL form applies. CGL coverage is denied to B. However, if employer B carries employers liability insurance, the third-party-over suit can be handled by that coverage.

There are other facets of the commercial general liability form that should be mentioned at this time.

CGL exclusion (e) does not apply to liability assumed by the insured under an insured contract. Using the example noted above, if the injured leased employee sues employer A for negligence in the manner of the leasing of the employee, and the lease agreement calls upon employer B to assume the tort liability of A, then the contractual coverage in the general liability policy of B would respond. It is therefore possible for employer B to provide workers compensation benefits plus general liability damages to the same employee for the same incident.

The current CGL form defines "employee" as including a "leased worker". This means that the CGL insurer does not want to provide general liability coverage for bodily injury to a leased worker. That leased worker is considered an employee of the named insured and, as such, is affected by the same exclusions (d) and (e) that preclude bodily injury coverage for a regular employee of the named insured. Bodily injury to a leased worker is meant to be covered under a workers compensation policy. Note that the term "leased worker" does not include a "temporary worker".

## Stop Gap Coverage

Employers liability insurance is normally part of the standard workers compensation policy. A problem arises when a standard workers compensation policy is not provided. This occurs when the workers compensation program is operated by a monopolistic state fund. In such cases, employers liability coverage is not offered by the state and a gap in coverage exists. *Stop gap* coverage plugs that gap.

Note first of all that stop gap coverage is not a substitute for workers compensation coverage. Stop gap coverage is designed only to provide liability insurance for an employer who is sued by an employee injured in the course of employment.

In monopolistic state fund jurisdictions, employers may be able to purchase stop gap coverage from private insurers (or they can self-insure the exposure). Stop gap coverage can mirror the employers liability coverage provided on the workers compensation policy. However, the terms are not automatically the same. Stop gap coverage is not a standardized policy and the insured needs to review the policy to be sure the needed coverage is being provided.

Guidelines provide for basic limits of liability of $100,000 each accident for bodily injury by accident; $100,000 each employee for bodily injury by disease; and $500,000 policy limit for bodily injury by disease. Higher limits are permitted. The premium is based on the workers compensation classifications and rates in the NCCI workers compensation manual.

Defense costs can also be provided by stop gap insurance. If an employee can sue an employer over work-related injuries, that lawsuit brings with it attorneys' fees and court costs—and stop gap can help defray those costs. Lawsuits brought by spouses or other family members of the injured employees for loss of consortium or services could be another item handled by stop gap coverage. And, dual capacity and third-party-over claims can likewise be subject matters for stop gap.

Stop gap coverage can be added as an endorsement to either a general liability or a workers compensation policy, depending on the underwriting guidelines of the insurer.

The NCCI stop gap endorsements for a workers compensation policy are outlined in Chapter 6; however, insurers can write their own versions of the coverage.

## Workers Compensation and Volunteers

Workers compensation was created to apply to injuries of employees suffered in the course of employment. A question often arises when a volunteer is injured. Are volunteers employees? If the volunteers are considered employees, then the workers compensation system will respond if they are injured while performing their services. Unfortunately, there is no absolute standard on the status of volunteers under the workers compensation system. An entity that uses volunteers needs to know whether courts or statutes in its particular state have addressed the question of compensability of injuries to volunteers.

The following cases offer just a few examples of judicial thinking on this issue.

In Colorado, the state supreme court faced the issue of whether a claimant was an employee when he was injured on voluntary ski patrol in *Aspen Highlands Skiing Corp. v. Apostolou*, 866 P.2d 1384 (Colo. 1994). Apostolou was employed as a part-time ski instructor. He volunteered for ski patrol in exchange for ski passes for his girlfriend. During patrol, Apostolou fell and injured his knee. He sought workers compensation benefits, but the employer said he was a volunteer and not entitled to benefits. The state supreme court cited the definition of employee in the workers compensation statute, that is, "any person in the service of any private corporation under any contract of hire, express or implied." The court noted that Apostolou had negotiated with the employer for the ski passes. Apostolou had obligated himself to work and the employer had obligated itself to provide free passes. This established a contractual relationship, meaning that Apostolou was an employee within the terms of the statute.

*Morales v. Workers' Compensation Appeals Board*, 186 Cal App.3d 283 (1986) was a case where a county prisoner doing community work was found to be an employee entitled to workers compensation benefits. Morales was sentenced to sixty days in jail and put in a voluntary community work program. There was no monetary compensation offered and no contractual negotiations. The only consideration Morales received was freedom from the physical confinement of a jail cell while doing community work. Morales hurt his back during the work and sought workers compensation benefits. The California appeals court decided that consideration other than wages may support a contract of hire within the meaning of the state workers compensation law. Therefore, since Morales had received consideration in the form of semi-freedom in exchange for his work, a work contract could be said to exist. This meant Morales could be considered as an employee and entitled to workers compensation benefits.

In *McCreery v. Covenant Presbyterian Church*, 400 S.E.2d 130 (S.C. 1990), McCreery volunteered to help build a church and was injured during this work. He sought workers compensation benefits; coverage was disputed. A court of appeals found that McCreery was a volunteer and not an employee because he was not paid any money and received no other consideration for his services. Even though the Supreme Court reversed the lower court's decision on other grounds, the finding that McCreery was not an employee subject to the workers compensation statute was not denied by the Supreme Court.

To a great degree, the question of volunteer as employee rests upon whether consideration is granted for services. This consideration can be monetary or otherwise, but it can be seen as the basis of a contract between the worker and the other party. This establishes an employer-employee relationship.

## Various Workers Compensation Doctrines

There are several legal theories relating to workers compensation that have been promulgated by courts throughout the country. These theories may affect coverage under the workers compensation system even though they are not all accepted in every state.

### The Positional Risk Doctrinee

The positional risk doctrine is a legal theory that proposes an employee injury may be said to arise out of his employment if the injury would not have occurred but for the fact that the conditions or obligations of the employment placed the employee in a position where he was injured by a neutral force. This neutral force must be one that is neither personal to the employee nor associated distinctly with the employment.

A common example of the positional risk doctrine is where a vehicle crashes through the building where the employee is working, injuring the employee. Some would argue that there is no causal connection between the employment and the injury. In jurisdictions that have adopted the positional risk doctrine, it is held that the employee was injured only because he was at work, in a position where he had to be because of his employment. Thus, workers compensation benefits should be paid. The doctrine declares that mere presence is enough if the injured employee would not have been injured otherwise. Jurisdictions that do not accept the positional risk doctrine emphasize the point that mere presence at the work place is not by itself enough to certify that an injury arose out of and in the course of employment.

The positional risk doctrine is a minority opinion in this country. An overwhelming majority of states require a *causal* connection. If a causal connection between the injury and the employment is disputed, such disputes are decided on a case-by-case basis, with the court taking several factors into consideration.

Foremost among these factors is the claimant's medical evidence. When an injured worker makes a workers compensation claim, it must be shown that the connection between the injury and the employment is based on reasonable medical probability. In other words, the employee must have a doctor report that the injury did (or most probably did) occur as a result of the employment.

Another factor is whether the activity was undertaken at the employer's request or order. The employer-employee relationship is determined on the *right to control*. The employer tells the employee what to do and how to do it. If the employee is injured in the process of complying with the employer's instructions, the employer cannot effectively deny that the injury was connected to work.

Additional factors considered are whether the employer either directly or indirectly compelled the employee's attendance at the place of injury and whether the employer benefited in some way by the employee's activity. If a workers compensation board or a court were to find that an employer *did* compel attendance or *did* benefit from the activity, the injury suffered by the employee will be declared work-related and the causal connection established.

Another example can be seen in *Zemis v. SCI Contractors, Inc./E.E. Black, Inc.*, 911 P.2d 77 (Haw. 1996). The supreme court of Hawaii discussed the positional risk doctrine in relation to an assault by one worker upon another. Zemis was involved in a car accident with the wife of a coworker. The coworker blamed Zemis for the accident and, two days later, confronted Zemis at the work site and hit him. Zemis sought workers compensation benefits; the employer denied the injury was in the course of employment. One of the theories put forth by Zemis was the positional risk doctrine. The state supreme court found in favor of the employer and pointed out that the positional risk doctrine applies only when the risk to the employee is neutral—that is neither personal to the claimant nor distinctly associated with the employment. In this case, the court decided that there was no reasonable inference that the nature of the employment created the risk.

## Odd Lot Doctrine

The odd lot doctrine allows the finding of permanent total disability when a relatively small percentage of impairment caused by a work-related accident is combined with other factors to render a claimant unable to obtain employment. The employee does not have to be completely physically disabled under this doctrine. Some of the other factors to be considered are the age, education, and mental capacity of the claimant, as well as the claimant's ability to be trained. If a workers compensation board, after hearing the facts of the case, decides that the employee cannot obtain work because those factors preclude it, then permanent total disability can be granted.

## Usual Exertion Doctrine

A majority of jurisdictions throughout the country apply the *usual exertion doctrine*. It states that an injury to an employee is compensable if the ordinary stress and strain of employment is shown to be a substantial cause of the injury. The unusual exertion rule requires a claimant to show that he was engaged in some form of unusual exertion or activity at the time of a job-related injury in order to collect workers compensation benefits.

These two principles usually come into play when disputes over workers compensation benefits arise because of preexisting conditions. For example, some would deny compensation to an employee who suffers a heart attack while on the job because that employee had a preexisting heart condition, unless it can be shown that the employee engaged in extraordinary or unusual exertion while working. Others support the idea that if an employee suffers a heart attack while engaged in the usual exertion of the job, compensation should be paid if a causal connection existed between the work-related activity and the injury; the presence of a preexisting problem or disorder is not the main point.

Neither the usual exertion principle nor the unusual exertion rule have any direct affect on the workers compensation policy. The policy agreement states that the insurer will pay promptly when due the benefits required by the workers compensation law. Therefore, if a particular state workers compensation law (or court) declares that compensation is due, the workers compensation policy will respond.

## Last Injurious Exposure Rule

Disputes may arise between employers or insurers over whether an injury is new or an aggravation of a prior injury. Under the *last injurious exposure rule*, it is the legal burden of the previous employer to show that the injury is a new one. If a new injury is proven, the current employer is responsible for compensation payments. If it is not proven, the previous employer may end up paying the compensation or splitting the payments, depending on how and to whom the workers compensation board apportions the injury.

Under this rule, if the current employer is ordered to make all the compensation payments, neither the employer nor its insurer is allowed to pursue the previous employer or its insurer for any contribution, unless state law permits such a course of action.

## Peculiar Risk Doctrine

The peculiar risk doctrine, which is also known as the special risk doctrine, holds that a person who hires an independent contractor to perform work that is inherently dangerous (a peculiar risk) can be held liable for tort damages when the contractor's negligent performance causes injuries to others. The reasoning behind the doctrine is that an innocent third party injured by the negligence of an independent contractor should not have to depend just on the contractor's ability to pay in order to receive compensation. Another source of compensation is the person who was to benefit from the contractor's work.

Such reasoning is not altogether unacceptable. Indeed, the owners and contractors protective liability coverage form is meant to apply to bodily injury and property damage arising out of operations performed for the named insured by a specified contractor. A problem arose, though, when some courts expanded the peculiar risk doctrine to allow a contractor's employees who were injured on the job through the negligence of the contractor to seek recovery from the person who hired the contractor, in addition to receiving workers compensation benefits.

A majority of courts around the country do not support this viewpoint— *Wagner v. Continental Casualty Co.*, 421 N.W.2d 835 (Wisc. 1988); *Peone v. Regulus Stud Mills*, 744 P.2d 102 (Idaho 1987); *Jones v. Chevron USA, Inc.*, 718 P.2d 890 (Wyo. 1986); and *Vertentes v. Barletta Co.*, 466 N.E.2d 500 (Mass. 1984). Also, in *Privette v. Superior Court of Santa Clara County*, 854 P.2d 721 (Cal. 1993), the California Supreme Court ruled that the peculiar risk doctrine provides no tort remedy against the person who hired the contractor for employees of that independent contractor who have been injured on the job through the negligence of the contractor.

## Personal Comfort Doctrine

As has been discussed, questions often arise about whether the employee is actually in the course of employment at the time of injury. For example, is an employee in the course of employment while visiting a coworker and talking about vacation plans? What about when the employee is on the phone talking to a relative? Are trips to the restroom just for personal grooming considered in the course of employment? Would workers compensation apply to injuries suffered under such circumstances?

These circumstances fit within the scope of the personal comfort doctrine. Virginia offers an example. *Kraf Construction Services, Inc. v.*

*Ingram*, 437 S.E.2d 424 (Va. Ct. App. 1993) was a case in which a construction worker was injured while crossing a street to get a soft drink at a convenience store. The worker filed for workers compensation benefits, and the employer fought against it, saying the employee was not in the course of employment or even on the work premises. A Virginia appeals court said that an employee who seeks to satisfy his personal comfort is within the employment. However, there are restrictions on this notion: the employee has to use the facilities furnished to him by the employer, and is not supposed to go someplace else. In the *Kraf* case, the employee was not on the employer's premises; however, going for a soft drink was held to be incidental to employment.

The Oregon Supreme Court and the Wisconsin Supreme Court have both considered the issue. In *Fred Meyer, Inc. v. Hayes,* 943 P.2d 197 (Ore. 1997), the Oregon Supreme Court asked the question: was the conduct of the employee expressly or impliedly allowed by the employer? If so, activities personal in nature are reasonably incidental to employment and injuries suffered by the employee are compensable. In *Sauerwein v. Department of Industry and Human Relations*, 262 N.W.2d 126 (Wisc. 1978), the Wisconsin Supreme Court stated that "employees who engage in acts which minister to personal comfort do not thereby leave the course of employment, unless the departure is so great that an intent to abandon the job temporarily may be inferred, or unless the method chosen is so unusual and unreasonable that the conduct cannot be considered as incident of the employment". The court went on to list some activities that it considered permissible within the personal comfort doctrine: getting a drink; eating lunch on the premises; warming oneself; sleeping in a place provided by the employer; going to the bathroom; and going to get paid.

The bottom line is that such activities have to be reasonable and not expressly forbidden by the employer.

## Successive Injury Cases

Forty-one states, three territories, and twelve Canadian provinces provide for second or subsequent injury funds as a means to encourage employers to hire disabled workers. The reason for this is that an individual who already is partially disabled may become totally disabled if injured on the job. Without a second injury fund, an employer—or its workers compensation carrier—could be responsible for the cost of a total disability when, in fact, the second occupational accident alone would not result in disability.

The second or subsequent injury fund pays the difference in benefits between the combined disability and the required benefits if only the occupational injury had occurred. For example, an individual who was born with one hand may be hired. If the employee loses that hand in an occupational accident, the employer would be responsible for benefits based on the combined loss of both hands. This is much higher than for just the loss of one hand.

Even when second injury funds are not involved, issues often arise over which employer or workers compensation carrier is responsible when an employee who was previously injured in an occupational accident is injured in a second accident. This often results in disagreement over whether the second injury is an *aggravation* of a pre-existing condition or the *recurrence* of an old injury. Such disagreements are common when there are different employers or different insurance carriers during the two incidents, as well as when second injury payments are being considered.

There may be variations among states but, in general, an aggravation of a pre-existing condition usually is considered a new injury. The employer of record at the time of the injury usually is held responsible for workers compensation coverage. A recurrence of an old injury usually reverts to the employer of record when the original injury happened.

In *Kidder v. Coastal Construction Co., Inc.*, 342 A.2d 729 (Me. 1975), the Maine Supreme Court considered an employee who was temporarily disabled by two successive injuries that occurred in two separate employment situations. The two injuries combined to produce a single indivisible disabling case. The court listed three possible methods to decide who was responsible:

1.  Apply the Massachusetts-Michigan rule and place full liability on the carrier at the time of the most recent injury that contributed to the disability
2.  Tap the second injury fund to pay the difference between permanent, total, and temporary partial disability
3.  Apportion the loss between the two insurers of record at the time of each injury

According to the Massachusetts-Michigan rule, liability is placed on the insurer that covers the risk at the time of the most recent injury that causally relates to the disability. In *Kidder,* the court ruled that each employer and respective carrier should pay equal portions of the disability benefits since each accident had contributed to the disabling condition.

# Appendices

# WORKERS COMPENSATION AND
# EMPLOYERS LIABILITY INSURANCE POLICY
# WC 00 00 01 A

Original Printing         Issued May 1, 1988         Standard

## INFORMATION PAGE

Insurer

| POLICY NO. |
| --- |

1. The Insured:                _____Individual        _____Partnership

   Mailing address:         _____Corporation or_____

2. The policy period is from _____ to _____ at the insured's mailing address.

3. A.   Workers Compensation Insurance: Part One of the policy applies to the Workers Compensation Law of the states listed here.:

   B.   Employers Liability Insurance: Part Two of the policy applies to work in  each state                                                 listed in Item 3.A. The limits of our liability under Part Two are:

   Bodily Injury by Accident      $_____ each accident
   Bodily Injury by Disease       $_____ policy limit
   Bodily Injury by Disease       $_____ each employee

   C.   Other States Insurance: Part Three of the policy applies to the states, if any, listed here:

   D.   This policy includes these endorsements and schedules:

4. The premium for this policy will be determined by our Manuals of Rules, Classifications, Rates and Rating Plans. All information required below is subject to verification and change by audit.

| Classifications | Code No | Premium Basis Total Estimated Annual Remuneration | Rate Per $100 of Remuneration | Estimated Annual Premium |
| --- | --- | --- | --- | --- |

Total Estimated Annual Premium $

Minimum Premium $                    Expense Constant $

Countersigned by _____

**Workers Compensation And Employers Liability Insurance Policy**          **WC 00 00 00 A**

**1st Reprint**                *Effective April 1, 1992*                **Standard**

### Workers Compensation And Employers Liability Insurance Policy

In return for the payment of the premium and subject to all terms ofthis policy, we agree with you as follows:

**GENERAL SECTION**

A. **The Policy**
This policy includes at its effective date the Information Page and all endorsements and schedules listed there. It is a contract of insurance between you (the employer named in Item 1 of the Information Page) and us (the insurer named on the Information Page). The only agreements relating to this insurance are stated in this policy. The terms of this policy may not be changed or waived except by endorsement issued by us to be part of this policy.

B. **Who Is Insured**
You are insured if you are an employer named in Item 1 of the Information Page. If that employer is a partnership, and if you are one of its partners, you are insured, but only in your capacity as an employer of the partnership's employees.

C. **Workers Compensation Law**
Workers Compensation Law means the workers or workmen's compensation law and occupational disease law of each state or territory named in Item 3.A. of the Information Page. It includes any amendments to that law which are in effect during the policy period. It does not include any federal workers or workmen's compensation law, any federal occupational disease law or the provisions of any law that provide nonoccupational disability benefits.

D. **State**
State means any state of the United States of America, and the District of Columbia.

E. **Locations**
This policy covers all of your workplaces listed in Items 1 or 4 of the Information Page; and it covers all other workplaces in Item 3.A. states unless you have other insurance or are self-insured for such workplaces.

### PART ONE
### WORKERS COMPENSATION INSURANCE

A. **How This Insurance Applies**
This workers compensation insurance applies to bodily injury by accident or bodily injury by disease. Bodily injury includes resulting death.
1. Bodily injury by accident must occur during the policy period.
2. Bodily injury by disease must be caused or aggravated by the conditions of your employment. The employee's last day of last exposure to the conditions causing or aggravating such bodily injury by disease must occur during the policy period.

B. **We Will Pay**
We will pay promptly when due the benefits required of you by the workers compensation law.

C. **We Will Defend**
We have the right and duty to defend at our expense any claim, proceeding or suit against you for benefits payable by this insurance. We have the right to investigate and settle these claims, proceedings or suits.

We have no duty to defend a claim, proceeding or suit that is not covered by this insurance.

D. **We Will Also Pay**
We will also pay these costs, in addition to other amounts payable under this insurance, as part of any claim, proceeding or suit we defend:
1. reasonable expenses incurred at our request, but not loss of earnings;
2. premiums for bonds to release attachments and for appeal bonds in bond amounts up to the amount payable under this insurance;
3. litigation costs taxed against you;
4. interest on a judgment as required by law until we offer the amount due under this insurance; and
5. expenses we incur.

E. **Other Insurance**
We will not pay more than our share of benefits and costs covered by this insurance and

### Workers Compensation And Employers Liability Insurance Policy

other insurance or self-insurance. Subject to any limits of liability that may apply, all shares will be equal until the loss is paid. If any insurance or self-insurance is exhausted, the shares of all remaining insurance will be equal until the loss is paid.

F.  **Payments You Must Make**
You are responsible for any payments in excess of the benefits regularly provided by the workers compensation law including those required because:
1. of your serious and willful misconduct;
2. you knowingly employ an employee in violation of law;
3. you fail to comply with a health or safety law or regulation; or
4. you discharge, coerce or otherwise discriminate against any employee in violation of the workers compensation law.

If we make any payments in excess of the benefits regularly provided by the workers compensation law on your behalf, you will reimburse us promptly.

G.  **Recovery From Others**
We have your rights, and the rights of persons entitled to the benefits of this insurance, to recover our payments from anyone liable for the injury. You will do everything necessary to protect those rights for us and to help us enforce them.

H.  **Statutory Provisions**
These statements apply where they are required by law.
1. As between an injured worker and us, we have notice of the injury when you have notice.
2. Your default or the bankruptcy or insolvency of you or your estate will not relieve us of our duties under this insurance after an injury occurs.
3. We are directly and primarily liable to any person entitled to the benefits payable by this insurance. Those persons may enforce our duties; so may an agency authorized by law. Enforcement may be against us or against you and us.
4. Jurisdiction over you is jurisdiction over us for purposes of the workers compensation law. We are bound by decisions against you under that law, subject to the provisions of this policy that are not in conflict with that law.
5. This insurance conforms to the parts

of the workers compensation law that apply to:
a. benefits payable by this insurance;
b. special taxes, payments into security or other special funds, and assessments payable by us under that law.
6. Terms of this insurance that conflict with the workers compensation law are changed by this statement to conform to that law.
Nothing in these paragraphs relieves you of your duties under this policy.

### PART TWO
### EMPLOYERS LIABILITY INSURANCE

A.  **How This Insurance Applies**
This employers liability insurance applies to bodily injury by accident or bodily injury by disease. Bodily injury includes resulting death.
1. The bodily injury must arise out of and in the course of the injured employee's employment by you.
2. The employment must be necessary or incidental to your work in a state or territory listed in Item 3.A. of the Information Page.
3. Bodily injury by accident must occur during the policy period.
4. Bodily injury by disease must be caused or aggravated by the conditions of your employment. The employee's last day of last exposure to the conditions causing or aggravating such bodily injury by disease must occur during the policy period.
5. If you are sued, the original suit and any related legal actions for damages for bodily injury by accident or by disease must be brought in the United States of America, its territories or possessions, or Canada.

B.  **We Will Pay**
We will pay all sums you legally must pay as damages because of bodily injury to your employees, provided the bodily injury is covered by this Employers Liability Insurance.
The damages we will pay, where recovery is permitted by law, include damages:
1. for which you are liable to a third party by reason of a claim or suit against you by that third party to recover the damages claimed

## Workers Compensation And Employers Liability Insurance Policy

against such third party as a result of injury to your employee;

2. for care and loss of services; and

3. for consequential bodily injury to a spouse, child, parent, brother or sister of the injured employee; provided that these damages are the direct consequence of bodily injury that arises out of and in the course of the injured employee's employment by you; and

4. because of bodily injury to your employee that arises out of and in the course of employment, claimed against you in a capacity other than as employer.

C. **Exclusions**

This insurance does not cover:

1. liability assumed under a contract. This exclusion does not apply to a warranty that your work will be done in a workmanlike manner;

2. punitive or exemplary damages because of bodily injury to an employee employed in violation of law;

3. bodily injury to an employee while employed in violation of law with your actual knowledge or the actual knowledge of any of your executive officers;

4. any obligation imposed by a workers compensation, occupational disease, unemployment compensation, or disability benefits law, or any similar law;

5. bodily injury intentionally caused or aggravated by you;

6. bodily injury occurring outside the United States of America, its territories or possessions, and Canada. This exclusion does not apply to bodily injury to a citizen or resident of the United States of America or Canada who is temporarily outside these countries;

7. damages arising out of coercion, criticism, demotion, evaluation, reassignment, discipline, defamation, harassment, humiliation, discrimination against or termination of any employee, or any personnel practices, policies, acts or omissions;

8. bodily injury to any person in work subject to the Longshore and Harbor Workers' Compensation Act (33 USC Sections 901-950), the Nonappropriated Fund Instrumentalities Act (5 USC Sections 8171-8173), the Outer Continental Shelf Lands Act (43 USC Sections 1331-1356), the Defense Base Act (42 USC Sections 1651-1654), the Federal Coal Mine Health and Safety Act of 1969 (30 USC Sections 901-942), any other federal workers or workmen's compensation law or other federal occupational disease law, or any amendments to these laws;

9. bodily injury to any person in work subject to the Federal Employers' Liability Act (45 USC Sections 51-60), any other federal laws obligating an employer to pay damages to an employee due to bodily injury arising out of or in the course of employment, or any amendments to those laws;

10. bodily injury to a master or member of the crew of any vessel;

11. fines or penalties imposed for violation of federal or state law; and

12. damages payable under the Migrant and Seasonal Agricultural Worker Protection Act (29 USC Sections 1801-1872) and under any other federal law awarding damages for violation of those laws or regulations issued thereunder, and any amendments to those laws.

D. **We Will Defend**

We have the right and duty to defend, at our expense, any claim, proceeding or suit against you for damages payable by this insurance. We have the right to investigate and settle these claims, proceedings and suits.

We have no duty to defend a claim, proceeding or suit that is not covered by this insurance. We have no duty to defend or continue defending after we have paid our applicable limit of liability under this insurance.

E. **We Will Also Pay**

We will also pay these costs, in addition to other amounts payable under this insurance, as part of any claim, proceeding, or suit we defend:

1. reasonable expenses incurred at our request, but not loss of earnings;

2. premiums for bonds to release attachments and for appeal bonds in bond amounts up to the limit of our liability under this insurance;

3. litigation costs taxed against you;

4. interest on a judgment as required by law until we offer the amount due under this insurance; and

5. expenses we incur.

Workers Compensation And Employers Liability Insurance Policy                    **WC 00 00 00 A**

<u>**1st Reprint**</u>                    *Effective April 1, 1992*                    <u>**Standard**</u>

### Workers Compensation And Employers Liability Insurance Policy

F. **Other Insurance**

We will not pay more than our share of damages and costs covered by this insurance and other insurance or self-insurance. Subject to any limits of liability that apply, all shares will be equal until the loss is paid. If any insurance or self-insurance is exhausted, the shares of all remaining insurance and self-insurance will be equal until the loss is paid.

G. **Limits of Liability**

Our liability to pay for damages is limited. Our limits of liability are shown in Item 3.B. of the Information Page. They apply as explained below.

1. Bodily Injury by Accident. The limit shown for "bodily injury by accident--each accident" is the most we will pay for all damages covered by this insurance because of bodily injury to one or more employees in any one accident.

A disease is not bodily injury by accident unless it results directly from bodily injury by accident.

2. Bodily Injury by Disease. The limit shown for "bodily injury by disease--policy limit" is the most we will pay for all damages covered by this insurance and arising out of bodily injury by disease, regardless of the number of employees who sustain bodily injury by disease. The limit shown for "bodily injury by disease--each employee" is the most we will pay for all damages because of bodily injury by disease to any one employee.

Bodily injury by disease does not include disease that results directly from a bodily injury by accident.

3. We will not pay any claims for damages after we have paid the applicable limit of our liability under this insurance.

H. **Recovery From Others**

We have your rights to recover our payment from anyone liable for an injury covered by this insurance. You will do everything necessary to protect those rights for us and to help us enforce them.

I. **Actions Against Us**

There will be no right of action against us under this insurance unless:

1. You have complied with all the terms of this policy; and

2. The amount you owe has been determined with our consent or by actual trial and final judgment.

This insurance does not give anyone the right to add us as a defendant in an action against you to determine your liability. The bankruptcy or insolvency of you or your estate will not relieve us of our obligations under this Part.

### PART THREE
### OTHER STATES INSURANCE

A. **How This Insurance Applies**

1. This other states insurance applies only if one or more states are shown in Item 3.C. of the Information Page.

2. If you begin work in any one of those states after the effective date of this policy and are not insured or are not self-insured for such work, all provisions of the policy will apply as though that state were listed in Item 3.A. of the Information Page.

3. We will reimburse you for the benefits required by the workers compensation law of that state if we are not permitted to pay the benefits directly to persons entitled to them.

4. If you have work on the effective date of this policy in any state not listed in Item 3.A. of the Information Page, coverage will not be afforded for that state unless we are notified within thirty days.

B. **Notice**

Tell us at once if you begin work in any state listed in Item 3.C. of the Information Page.

### PART FOUR
### YOUR DUTIES IF INJURY OCCURS

Tell us at once if injury occurs that may be covered by this policy. Your other duties are listed here.

1. Provide for immediate medical and other services required by the workers compensation law.

2. Give us or our agent the names and addresses of the injured persons and of witnesses, and other information we may need.

3. Promptly give us all notices, demands and legal papers related to the injury, claim, proceeding or suit.

### Workers Compensation And Employers Liability Insurance Policy

4.  Cooperate with us and assist us, as we may request, in the investigation, settlement or defense of any claim, proceeding or suit.
5.  Do nothing after an injury occurs that would interfere with our right to recover from others.
6.  Do not voluntarily make payments, assume obligations or incur expenses, except at your own cost.

### PART FIVE--PREMIUM

A.  **Our Manuals2**
All premium for this policy will be determined by our manuals of rules, rates, rating plans and classifications. We may change our manuals and apply the changes to this policy if authorized by law or a governmental agency regulating this insurance.

B.  **Classifications**
Item 4 of the Information Page shows the rate and premium basis for certain business or work classifications. These classifications were assigned based on an estimate of the exposures you would have during the policy period. If your actual exposures are not properly described by those classifications, we will assign proper classifications, rates and premium basis by endorsement to this policy.

C.  **Remuneration**
Premium for each work classification is determined by multiplying a rate times a premium basis. Remuneration is the most common premium basis. This premium basis includes payroll and all other remuneration paid or payable during the policy period for the services of:
1.  all your officers and employees engaged in work covered by this policy; and
2.  all other persons engaged in work that could make us liable under Part One (Workers Compensation Insurance) of this policy. If you do not have payroll records for these persons, the contract price for their services and materials may be used as the premium basis. This paragraph 2 will not apply if you give us proof that the employers of these persons lawfully secured their workers compensation obligations.

D.  **Premium Payments**
You will pay all premium when due. You will pay the premium even if part or all of a workers compensation law is not valid.

E.  **Final Premium**
The premium shown on the Information Page, schedules, and endorsements is an estimate. The final premium will be determined after this policy ends by using the actual, not the estimated, premium basis and the proper classifications and rates that lawfully apply to the business and work covered by this policy. If the final premium is more than the premium you paid to us, you must pay us the balance. If it is less, we will refund the balance to you. The final premium will not be less than the highest minimum premium for the classifications covered by this policy.
If this policy is canceled, final premium will be determined in the following way unless our manuals provide otherwise:
1.  If we cancel, final premium will be calculated pro rata based on the time this policy was in force. Final premium will not be less than the pro rata share of the minimum premium.
2.  If you cancel, final premium will be more than pro rata; it will be based on the time this policy was in force, and increased by our short-rate cancellation table and procedure. Final premium will not be less than the minimum premium.

F.  **Records**
You will keep records of information needed to compute premium. You will provide us with copies of those records when we ask for them.

G.  **Audit**
You will let us examine and audit all your records that relate to this policy. These records include ledgers, journals, registers, vouchers, contracts, tax reports, payroll and disbursement records, and programs for storing and retrieving data. We may conduct the audits during regular business hours during the policy period and within three years after the policy period ends. Information developed by audit will be used to determine final premium. Insurance rate service organizations have the same rights we have under this provision.

Workers Compensation And Employers Liability Insurance Policy        **WC 00 00 00 A**

__1st Reprint__        _Effective April 1, 1992_        __Standard__

**Workers Compensation And Employers Liability Insurance Policy**

### PART SIX--CONDITIONS

A.  **Inspection**

We have the right, but are not obliged to inspect your workplaces at any time. Our inspections are not safety inspections. They relate only to the insurability of the workplaces and the premiums to be charged. We may give you reports on the conditions we find. We may also recommend changes. While they may help reduce losses, we do not undertake to perform the duty of any person to provide for the health or safety of your employees or the public. We do not warrant that your workplaces are safe or healthful or that they comply with laws, regulations, codes or standards. Insurance rate service organizations have the same rights we have under this provision.

B.  **Long Term Policy**

If the policy period is longer than one year and sixteen days, all provisions of this policy will apply as though a new policy were issued on each annual anniversary that this policy is in force.

C.  **Transfer of Your Rights and Duties**

Your rights or duties under this policy may not be transferred without our written consent.

If you die and we receive notice within thirty days after your death, we will cover your legal representative as insured.

D.  **Cancelation**

1.  You may cancel this policy. You must mail or deliver advance written notice to us stating when the cancelation is to take effect.

2.  We may cancel this policy. We must mail or deliver to you not less than ten days advance written notice stating when the cancelation is to take effect. Mailing that notice to you at your mailing address shown in Item 1 of the Information Page will be sufficient to prove notice.

3.  The policy period will end on the day and hour stated in the cancelation notice.

4.  Any of these provisions that conflict with a law that controls the cancelation of the insurance in this policy is changed by this statement to comply with the law.

E.  **Sole Representative**

The insured first named in Item 1 of the Information Page will act on behalf of all insureds to change this policy, receive return premium, and give or receive notice of cancelation.

# WORKERS COMPENSATION EXPERIENCE RATING

NAME                             RISK IDENT. NO. 1111111          EFFECTIVE DATE 7/1/95
OF                               STATE FLORIDA
RISK ABLE MANUFACTURING

| 1 CODE | 2 ELR | 3 D-RATIO | 4 PAYROLL | 5 EXPECTED LOSSES | 6 EXP PRIM LOSSES | 7 CLAIM DATA | 8 IJ | O F | 9 ACT INC LOSSES | 10 ACT PRIM LOSSES |
|---|---|---|---|---|---|---|---|---|---|---|
| **INSURER 123** | | | **POLICY NO. 92** | | **EFF-DATE 1/1/91** | **EXP-DATE 1/1/92** | | | | |
| 0083 | 6.90 | 0.25 | 2,100,000 | 144,900 | 36,225 | 123456-92 | 5 | F | 295,000 # | 5,000 |
| 0035 | 2.00 | 0.26 | 500,000 | 10,000 | 2,600 | | | * | 4,000 | 4,000 |
| 3383 | 1.40 | 0.25 | 220,000 | 3,080 | 770 | | | | | |
| 8810 | 0.28 | 0.25 | 300,000 | 840 | 210 | | | | | |
| POLICY - TOTAL | | | 3,120,000 | | (SUBJECT PREMIUM = 249,600) | | | | 110,500 | 9,000 |
| **INSURER 123** | | | **POLICY NO. 93** | | **EFF-DATE 1/1/92** | **EXP-DATE 1/1/93** | | | | |
| 0083 | 6.90 | 0.25 | 2,250,000 | 155,250 | 38,813 | 123456-93 | 1 | 0 | 113,500 # | 5,000 |
| 0035 | 2.00 | 0.26 | 550,000 | 11,000 | 2,860 | 123457-93 | 5 | 0 | 6,000 | 5,000 |
| 3383 | 1.40 | 0.25 | 200,000 | 2,800 | 700 | | | * | 1,300 | 1,300 |
| 8810 | 0.28 | 0.25 | 340,000 | 952 | 238 | | | | | |
| POLICY - TOTAL | | | 3,340,000 | | (SUBJECT PREMIUM = 267,200) | | | | 113,800 | 11,300 |
| **INSURER 123** | | | **POLICY NO. 94** | | **EFF-DATE 1/1/93** | **EXP-DATE 1/1/94** | | | | |
| 0083 | 6.90 | 0.25 | 2,220,500 | 153,215 | 38,304 | 123456-94 | 1 | F | 74,000 | 5,000 |
| 0035 | 2.00 | 0.26 | 545,000 | 10,900 | 2,834 | 123457-94 | 5 | F | 23,000 | 5,000 |
| 3383 | 1.40 | 0.25 | 158,000 | 2,212 | 553 | | | * | 5,000 | 5,000 |
| 8810 | 0.28 | 0.25 | 275,000 | 770 | 193 | | | | | |
| POLICY - TOTAL | | | 3,198,500 | | (SUBJECT PREMIUM = 255,880) | | | | 102,000 | 15,000 |
| (A) | (B) EXPECTED | (C) EXCESS (D-E) | (D) | (E) ACTUAL | (F) EXCESS (H-I) | (G) | (H) | (I) | | |
| 0.33 | | 371,620 | 495,919 | 124,299 | 255,700 | 59,500 | 326,300 | 70,600 | | |

*Total by Policy Year of all cases $2,00 or less
#Limited loss

| | | (11)PRIMARY LOSSES | (12) STABLIZING VALUE | (13)RATABLE EXCESS | (14) TOTALS | |
|---|---|---|---|---|---|---|
| PAGE NUMBER | ACTUAL | (1) 70,600 | (C)x(1-W)+G 308,485 | (A)x(F) 84,381 | (J) 463,466 | |
| DATE | EXPECTED | (B) 124,299 | 308,485 | (A)x(C) 122,635 | (K) 555,419 | (15) EXP MOD (J)/(K) 0.83 |

## ERM-14 FORM—CONFIDENTIAL REQUEST FOR OWNERSHIP INFORMATION
*Effective 01 Dec 2003*

**All items must be answered completely or the form may be returned.**

The following confidential ownership statements may be used only in establishing premiums for your insurance coverages. Your workers compensation policy requires that you report ownership changes, and other changes as detailed below, to your insurance carrier in writing within 90 days of the change. If you have questions, contact your agent, insurance company, or the appropriate rating organization. Once completed, this form must be submitted to the rating organization by you, your insurance carrier(s), or your agents. If this form does not provide the means to explain the transaction, enter as much information on the form as possible and supplement the form with a narrative on the employer's letterhead, signed by an owner, partner, or executive officer.

### Section A—Transaction and Entity Information

| Check all that apply | Type of Transaction Columns A, B, and C referenced below are found in Section B. | Effective Date Enter effective date of transaction | Reported Date Enter date reported in writing to your insurance provider |
|---|---|---|---|
| | **Name and/or legal entity change**—Complete column A for former entity and column B for newly named entity. Complete Type of Entity portion for each entity to reflect such change. | | |
| | **Sale, transfer or conveyance of all or a portion of an entity's ownership interest**—Complete column A for ownership before the change and column B for ownership after the change. | | |
| | **Sale, transfer or conveyance of an entity's physical assets to another entity that takes over its operations**—Complete column A for the former entity and column B for the acquiring entity. | | |
| | **Merger or consolidation (attach copy of agreement)**—Complete columns A and B for the former entities and column C for the surviving entity. | | |
| | **Formation of a new entity that acts as, or in effect is, a successor to another entity that:** (a) Has dissolved (b) Is non-operative (c) May continue to operate in a limited capacity. | | |
| | **An irrevocable trust or receiver, established either voluntarily or by court mandate**—Complete column A before the change and column B after the change. | | |
| | **Determination of combinability of separate entities**—Complete a separate column in Section B for each entity to be reviewed for common ownership (attach additional forms if necessary). | | |

### ENTITY 1—Complete Column A on Page 3

**Complete Name of Entity** (including DBA or TA) _____

**Risk ID** _____    FEIN _____

**Type of Entity** (check all that apply)    Carrier _____    Policy # _____    Eff. Date _____

☐ Sole Proprietorship       ☐ Limited Partnership              ☐ Temporary Labor Service    ☐ School District     ☐ Irrevocable Trust
☐ Partnership               ☐ Limited Liability Corporation    ☐ Publicly Traded            ☐ For Profit          ☐ Religious Organization
☐ Domestic Corporation      ☐ Joint Venture                    ☐ State Agency               ☐ Not for Profit      ☐ Charitable Organization
☐ Foreign Corporation       ☐ Association (including unincorporated)    ☐ County Agency       ☐ Non-Profit          ☐ Franchise
☐ Sub-Chapter S-Corp        ☐ Employee Leasing                 ☐ Municipality               ☐ Revocable Trust     ☐ ESOP

**Primary Address**

Street _____    City, State, Zip _____

Telephone Number _____    Fax Number _____    E-mail Address _____

Contact Name _____    Web Site _____

Mailing Address (if different than Primary Address) _____

Additional Location(s) _____

**ERM-14 (Rev. 12/03)**                                                                                     **NC790**

Page 1 of 4

## ENTITY 2—Complete Column B on Page 3

**Complete Name of Entity** (including DBA or TA) _____

**Risk ID** _____    FEIN _____

**Type of Entity** (check all that apply)   Carrier _____   Policy # _____   Eff. Date _____

☐ Sole Proprietorship   ☐ Limited Partnership   ☐ Temporary Labor Service   ☐ School District   ☐ Irrevocable Trust
☐ Partnership   ☐ Limited Liability Corporation   ☐ Publicly Traded   ☐ For Profit   ☐ Religious Organization
☐ Domestic Corporation   ☐ Joint Venture   ☐ State Agency   ☐ Not for Profit   ☐ Charitable Organization
☐ Foreign Corporation   ☐ Association (including unincorporated)   ☐ County Agency   ☐ Non-Profit   ☐ Franchise
☐ Sub-Chapter S-Corp   ☐ Employee Leasing   ☐ Municipality   ☐ Revocable Trust   ☐ ESOP

**Primary Address**

Street _____   City, State, Zip _____

Telephone Number _____   Fax Number _____   E-mail Address _____

Contact Name _____   Web Site _____

Mailing Address (if different than Primary Address) _____

Additional Location(s) _____

## ENTITY 3—Complete Column C on Page 3

**Complete Name of Entity** (including DBA or TA) _____

**Risk ID** _____    FEIN _____

**Type of Entity** (check all that apply)   Carrier _____   Policy # _____   Eff. Date _____

☐ Sole Proprietorship   ☐ Limited Partnership   ☐ Temporary Labor Service   ☐ School District   ☐ Irrevocable Trust
☐ Partnership   ☐ Limited Liability Corporation   ☐ Publicly Traded   ☐ For Profit   ☐ Religious Organization
☐ Domestic Corporation   ☐ Joint Venture   ☐ State Agency   ☐ Not for Profit   ☐ Charitable Organization
☐ Foreign Corporation   ☐ Association (including unincorporated)   ☐ County Agency   ☐ Non-Profit   ☐ Franchise
☐ Sub-Chapter S-Corp   ☐ Employee Leasing   ☐ Municipality   ☐ Revocable Trust   ☐ ESOP

**Primary Address**

Street _____   City, State, Zip _____

Telephone Number _____   Fax Number _____   E-mail Address _____

Contact Name _____   Web Site _____

Mailing Address (if different than Primary Address) _____

Additional Location(s) _____

## Section B—Ownership

1. Have any of these entities operated under another name in the last four years? ☐ Yes  ☐ No

2. Are any of the entities **currently** related through common majority ownership to any entity not listed on the front of the form? ☐ Yes  ☐ No

3. Have any of these entities been **previously** related through common majority ownership to any other entities in the last four years?
   ☐ Yes  ☐ No

4. If you answered Yes to questions 1, 2, or 3 above, provide additional information, indicating which question(s) your answer references:
   ☐ 1  ☐ 2  ☐ 3

| Name of Business | Principal Location | Carrier and Policy Number | Effective Date |
|---|---|---|---|
|  |  |  |  |
|  |  |  |  |

5. Were the assets and/or ownership interest (all or a portion) of this entity acquired from a previously existing business? ☐ Yes  ☐ No
   If yes, you must provide complete ownership information for the prior owner in column A and ownership information for the new owner in column B.

6. If this is a partial sale, transfer, or conveyance of an existing business (i.e., sale of one or more plants or locations):
   a. Explain what portion or location of the entire operation was sold, transferred, or conveyed.

   _____

   b. Was this entity insured under a separate policy from the remaining portion? ☐ Yes  ☐ No
   If not, specify the entities with which it was combined:

   _____

ERM-14 (Rev. 12/03)                                                                 NC790

7. Did the legal status of this entity change? ☐ Yes   ☐ No
   If yes, you must complete the Type of Entity portion for each entity to reflect such change.

8. Is this transaction a result of bankruptcy? ☐ Yes   ☐ No
   If yes, please indicate under which Chapter the bankruptcy was filed. _____

**Corporations**—List all names of owners of 5% or more of voting stock and number of shares owned. Submit shareholder proposal if transaction involved exchange of stock.

**Partnerships**—List each partner and appropriate share in the profits. If the entity is a limited partnership, list name(s) of each general partner(s).

**Other**—If no voting stock, list members of board of directors or comparable governing body.

| Information | Column A | Column B | Column C |
|---|---|---|---|
| | Enter name used in Section A for Entity 1 **Entity 1** | Enter name used in Section A for Entity 2 **Entity 2** | Enter name used in Section A for Entity 3 **Entity 3** If applicable, use this column for multiple combinations or entities resulting from mergers and consolidations |
| **Name of Entity** | | | |
| **Ownership** See reference above to ownership information required for corporations, partnerships, and other entities. | | | |
| **Total Ownership Interest or Number of Shares** | | | |

**NOTE:** If your business has changed significantly to result in a change to the primary (governing) classification and the process and hazard of the operation have also changed, contact your agent, insurance company or rating organization for additional information.

## Section C—Additional Information

Please include any additional information you believe pertinent to the transaction detailed above that cannot be expressed due to the format of this form. If there is not enough space below, attach the information on the entity's letterhead, signed by an owner, partner, or executive officer.

_____

_____

_____

_____

_____

ERM-14 (Rev. 12/03)                                    NC790

## Section D—Did You Remember to . . .

- Indicate the type of transaction, check all that apply, and include transaction and notification dates?
- Complete all necessary entity information? **Note:** You can use more forms if the number of entities exceeds three.
    - Entity name
    - Risk identification number (if you know it)
    - Federal Employer Identification Number (FEIN)
    - Type of entity
    - Primary address, telephone, and other contact information
    - Mailing address and additional locations if applicable
- Fill out the ownership table completely?
    - Include the names of the entities as listed in Section A?
    - Include all owners, partners, board of director members, members and/or manager of LLCs, general partners of LPs, or any other comparable governing body?
    - Include percentage of ownership for each owner, partner, board of director member, member and/or manager of LLCs, general partner of LPs, or any other comparable governing body?
- Answer questions 1 though 8?

## Section E—Certification

**This is to certify that the information contained on this form is complete and correct.**

**All forms will be returned if this Certification Section is incomplete.**

Name of person completing form:_____

Check which entity or entities the signer represents:    ☐Entity 1  ☐Entity 2  ☐Entity 3  ☐Other _____

| | | |
|---|---|---|
| Signature of Owner, Partner, Member, or Executive Officer | Title | Carrier |
| Print name of above signature | Date | Carrier Address |

## Section F—For Rating Organization Use Only

Associate/automated _____

Date received _____

Date complete _____

Assessment—form complete? What is missing? _____

Ruling _____

Revisions necessary—Yes/No _____

Revisions complete and mailed—Yes/No/NA _____

Rating Effective Date impacted—Yes/No—if Yes, which ones? _____

Risk ID impacted—list all impacted, any deactivated?  Indicate deactivated #s _____

All carriers/rating organizations notified? _____

**ERM-14 (Rev. 12/03)**                                                                                   **NC790**

**Page 4 of 4**

# Application of Workers Compensation Laws

| State | Exclusive Remedy[1] | Executive Officers[2] | Partners[3] | Sole Proprietors[4] | Agricultural Workers[5] | Domestic Employees[6] | Statutory Reference |
|-------|:---:|:---:|:---:|:---:|:---:|:---:|---|
| | | | | | | | **Who is Covered** (spanning) |
| Alabama | x | x | | | | | §25-5-50, 25-5-52 |
| Alaska | x | x | | | x | x | §23.30.239, 23.30.240, 23.30.055 |
| Arizona | | x | | | x | | §23-901, 23-1022, 23-1024 |
| Arkansas | x | x | x | x | | | §11-9-102, 11-9-105 |
| California | x | x | | | x | x | Labor Code §3351, 3602 |
| Colorado | x | x | | | x | x | §8-41-104, 8-41-202, 8-40-302 |
| Connecticut | x | x | x | | x | x | §31-275, 31-284 |
| Delaware | x | x | | | x | x | Tit. 19, §2304, 2308 |
| District of Columbia | x | x | | | x | x | §32-1504, §36-304 |
| Florida | x | x | | | x | | §440.02, 440.11 |
| Georgia | x | x | | | x | | §34-9-2.2, 34-9-11 |
| Hawaii | x | x | | | x | x | §386-4, 386-5 |
| Idaho | x | x | | | x | | §72-209,72-212, 72-213 |
| Illinois | x | x | | | x | x | Tit. 820, § 305/1, 305/5 |
| Indiana | x | x | | | | | §22-3-2-6, 22-3-6-1 |
| Iowa | x | x | | | x | x | §85.1, 85.1A, 85.20 |
| Kansas | x | x | | | | x | §44-501, 44-508 |
| Kentucky | x | x | | | | x | §342.012, 342.640, 342.690 |
| Louisiana | x | x | x | x | x | | §23:1032, 23:1035 |
| Maine | x | x | | | x | | Tit. 39-A, §34-A-401 |
| Maryland | x | x | | | x | x | Labor and Employment Code §9-206, 9-219, 9-227, 9-509 |
| Mass. | | x | | | x | x | Ch.152 §1, 24 |
| Michigan | x | x | x | | x | x | §17.237 |
| Minnesota | x | x | | | x | x | §176.031, 176.041 |
| Mississippi | x | x | | | | | §71-3-5, 71-3-9 |
| Missouri | x | x | | | x | | §287.030, 287.035, 287.120 |
| Montana | x | x | | | x | | §39-71-118, 39-71-411 |
| Nebraska | x | x | | | | | §48-110, 48-115 |
| Nevada | x | x | | | | x | §616A.020, 616A.105 |
| New Hampshire | x | x | | | x | x | §281-A:2, 281-A:8 |
| New Jersey | x | x | | | x | x | §34:15-8, 34:15-36 |
| New Mexico | x | x | | x | | | §52-1-6 |
| New York | x | x | | | x | x | Workers Compensation Law §2,11 |
| N. Carolina | x | x | | | x | x | §97-2, 97-10.1 |
| N. Dakota | x | | | | | | §65-01-02, 65-01-08 |
| Ohio | x | x | | | x | x | §4123.01, 4123.74 |
| Oklahoma | x | x | | | x | x | Tit. 85, §3, 12 |
| Oregon | x | x | | | x | | §656.018, 656.027, 656.128 |
| Pennsylvania | x | x | | | x | | Tit. 77, §481 |
| Rhode Island | x | x | | | | | §28-29-2, 28-29-20 |

| State | Exclusive Remedy[1] | Executive Officers[2] | Partners[3] | Sole Proprietors[4] | Agricultural Workers[5] | Domestic Employees[6] | Statutory Reference |
|---|---|---|---|---|---|---|---|
| | | | | Who is Covered | | | |
| S. Carolina | x | x | | | | x | §42-1-130, 42-1-540 |
| S. Dakota | x | x | | | x | x | §62-1-2, 62-1-7, 62-3-2 |
| Tennessee | x | x | | | | | §50-6-102, 50-6-108 |
| Texas | x | x | x | x | x | | Labor Code §406.097, 408.001 |
| Utah | x | x | | | x | x | §34A-2-104, 34A-2-105 |
| Vermont | x | x | | | x | | Tit. 21, §601, 622 |
| Virginia | x | x | | | x | | §65.2-101, 65.2-307 |
| Washington | x | x | | | x | x | §51.12.020, 51.32.010 |
| W.Virginia | x | x | x | x | x | | §23-2-1, 23-2-6 |
| Wisconsin | x | x | | | x | | §102.03, 102.075, 102.076 |
| Wyoming | x | | | | x | | §27-14-102, 27-14-104 |

[1] Some states allow employees to opt out of the workers compensation system. Some jurisdictions also allow employees to sue their employers for injuries or death arising from willful conduct, physical assault, fraudulent concealment, sexual harassment, sexual assault, defective products made by employers, invasion of privacy, infliction of emotional distress, or gross negligence.

[2] Although executive officers are subject to workers compensation in most states, some states allow officers to be exempt from workers compensation coverage.

[3] Partners are not subject to workers compensation in most states, but many jurisdictions allow partners to elect coverage. A few states that subject partners to workers compensation allow them to choose exemption.

[4] Sole proprietors are not generally subject to workers compensation, but most states allow them to elect coverage. A few states that require coverage allow sole proprietors to choose exemption.

[5] Some jurisdictions cover agricultural workers the same as other employees; some carry specific limitations.

[6] Many stipulations apply to coverage for domestic employees.

# Residual Market Systems

The following states use Assigned Risk Plans (Pools):

| | | |
|---|---|---|
| Alabama | Michigan | Vermont |
| Alaska | Minnesota | Virginia |
| Arizona | Mississippi | Wisconsin |
| Arkansas | Missouri | |
| Connecticut | Nebraska | |
| Delaware | Nevada | |
| District of Columbia | New Hampshire | |
| Georgia | New Jersey | |
| Idaho | New Mexico | |
| Illinois | North Carolina | |
| Indiana | Oregon | |
| Iowa | South Carolina | |
| Kansas | South Dakota | |
| Massachusetts | Tennessee | |

These states use the state fund:

| | |
|---|---|
| California | Ohio |
| Colorado | Oklahoma |
| Hawaii | Pennsylvania |
| Kentucky | Rhode Island |
| Louisiana | Texas |
| Maine | Utah |
| Maryland | Washington |
| Montana | West Virginia |
| New York | Wyoming |
| North Dakota | |

Florida uses a Joint Underwriting Association.

# Successive Injury Funds

| State | Covered Injuries | Employer Obligation | Fund Obligation | Fund Sources | Other Provisions |
|-------|------------------|---------------------|-----------------|--------------|------------------|
| Alabama | | | Successive Injury Fund Eliminated | | |
| Alaska Statutory ref: 23.30.040; 23.30.205 | Second injury which, when combined with pre-existing permanent impairment, results in greater disability than from second injury alone. | 104 weeks of disability resultant from second impairment | Excess of 104 weeks | Compensation up to 6% paid to fund; no-dependents death cases - $10,000; civil penalties | "Permanent impairment" as shown, or would support award of 200 weeks or more. |
| Arizona Stat. ref: 23-1065 | Second injury, combined with pre-existing work-related disability or non-industrially related physical impairment, which results in disability of work. | Resultant disability from second injury | Fund and employer are equally responsible for remaining difference between compensation for second injury and combined disability | Cost of self-insurance and 1.5% of all premiums. Up to 0.5% of yearly premiums may be allocated to fund to keep it sound | Employer must know of existing nonindustrial physical impairment |
| Arkansas Stat. ref: 11-9-525 | Second injury which when combined with previous partial impairment or disability, results in greater disability/impairment than from second injury alone. | Resultant disability from second injury | Difference between compensation for second injury and previous permanent disability. | A portion of premium tax is allocated to the Second Injury Fund; the Permanent Total Disability and Death fund receives $500 from no-dependency death cases. | |
| California Labor Code 4751, 62.5 | Second permanent partial injury, when combined with a pre-existing permanent partial disability, and results in 70% or more permanent disability. Unless prior injury involved a major member and second injury is to the opposite and corresponding member for at least 5%, second injury must account for 35% of disability. | Resultant disability from second injury | Difference between compensation for most recent injury and permanent total disability. | Legislative appropriations from nonadministrative expenses of the workers compensation program. | |
| Colorado | | | Successive Injury Fund Eliminated | | |
| Connecticut | | | Successive Injury Fund Eliminated | | |
| Delaware Stat. ref: Title 19, § 2327 | Disease or second injury which, when added to any pre-existing permanent injury, results in permanent total disability | Resultant disability from second injury | Difference between compensation for second injury and permanent total disability. | Premium received by insurance carriers is taxed at 2%. | |
| District of Columbia | | | Successive Injury Fund Eliminated | | |
| Florida | | | Successive Injury Fund Eliminated | | |

| State | Covered Injuries | Employer Obligation | Fund Obligation | Fund Sources | Other Provisions |
|-------|-----------------|---------------------|-----------------|--------------|------------------|
| Georgia Stat. ref: 34-9-241, 34-9-360 | Disease or second injury which, when combined with pre-existing permanent impairment, results in greater disability than from second injury alone. | Resultant disability from second injury for first 102 weeks. | Income benefits over 104 weeks; for medical and rehabilitation expenses from $5000 to $10,000 are reimbursed to employer at 50%. Medical and rehabilitation expenses above $10,000 are reimbursed at 100%. | Carriers and self-insureds are proportionately assessed up to 175% of disbursements from fund to annual compensation benefits paid, less net assets in fund. | Employer must know of prior impairment before second injury occurs. When no funds are needed assessments may be suspended or reduced. |
| Hawaii Stat ref: HRS 386-33, 386-151 | Second injury which when added to previous permanent partial disability results in permanent total disability or greater permanent partial disability | Resultant disability for the first 104 weeks | Benefits beyond the first 104 weeks | Assessments on insurers and self-insurers, plus a percentage of maximum weekly benefit rate in no-dependency death cases and the unpaid balance in permanent total and permanent partial disability cases with no depedents. | |
| Idaho Stat. ref: 72-332 | Second injury when added with prior permanent physical impairment causes permanent total disability. | Resultant disability from the second injury. | Difference between compensation for second injury and permanent disability. | Assessments based on semi-annual reporting of indemnity payments paid, not less than $200. | |
| Illinois Stat. ref: 820 ILCS 305/7 and 305/8 | Second injury involving loss of use of major members or loss of eye, when combined with pre-existing loss of member, causes permanent total disability. | Resultant disability from the second injury. | Difference between compensation for second injury and permanent. disability. | Employers contribute a percentage of compensation payments. | Payments are not required when the funds reach $600,000; reduced by half when the fund is at $500,000. Payments increase or are reinstated when the fund reaches $300,000 or $400,000. |
| Indiana Stat. ref: 22-3-3-13 | Second injury involving loss or loss of use of foot, leg arm, hand or eye, when combined with a pre-existing loss or loss of use or member, results in a permanent total disability. | Resultant disability from second injury. | Difference between compensation for second injury and permanent total disability. | Throughout the calendar year 25% of all benefits to injured employees is paid into the fund. An assessment may be charged if the fund drops below $1,000,000 on or before October 1. | |

| State | Covered Injuries | Employer Obligation | Fund Obligation | Fund Sources | Other Provisions |
|---|---|---|---|---|---|
| Iowa Stat. ref: 85.64-65 | Second injury involving loss of use of member or loss of eye, when combined with pre-existing loss of member, causes permanent disability. | Resultant disability from second injury | Difference between compensation for second injury and permanent disability, less the value of the previously lost member or organ. | Dependent death cases - $12,000; no-dependent death cases – $45,000. Payments due but not paid to nonresident alien dependents. | |
| Kansas | Successive Injury Fund Eliminated | | | | |
| Kentucky | Successive Injury Fund Eliminated | | | | |
| Louisiana Stat ref: 23-10:1378 | Second injury, when combined with known prior permanent partial disability, results in substantially greater disability or death than from second injury alone. Or second injury would not have occurred if not for pre-existing permanent partial disability. | Complete disability for the first 104 weeks; 175 weeks for death. | Reimburses employer for weekly compensation after the first 104 weeks, or 175 weeks in cases of death. | Assessments on carriers and self-insurers. | If no assessment payment is made there is no reimbursement. |
| Maine | Successive Injury Fund Eliminated | | | | |
| Maryland Stat. ref: 10-204 | Second injury, when added with pre-existing permanent impairment due to disease, congenital condition or accident, causes a greater combined disability constituting an impediment to employment. Total disability must be 50% of body or equivalent as a whole. | Resultant disability from second injury. | Additional compensation to employee if permanent disability resulting from prior and subsequent impairment exceeds 50% of the body as a whole. Prior and second injuries must each be compensable for at least 125 weeks. | A percentage of compensation on all awards and settlement agreements. | |
| Massachusetts Stat. ref: Title 21 152 § 65 | Second injury, when added to pre-existing physical impairment which results in substantially greater disability of death. | Disability benefits for the first 104 weeks | After the first 104 weeks the employer is reimbursed for up to 75% of benefits. | Employer assessment. | |
| Michigan Stat. ref: 418.521, 351-9 | Second injury which involves loss of eye or member, when added to pre-existing loss of eye or member, results in permanent total disability. | Resultant disability from second injury. | Difference between payment for second injury and permanent total disability. | Carrier and self-insurer assessments. | Fund is credited with balance above $200,000. |

| State | Covered Injuries | Employer Obligation | Fund Obligation | Fund Sources | Other Provisions |
|---|---|---|---|---|---|
| Minnesota | | Successive Injury Fund Eliminated | | | |
| Mississippi Stat. ref: 71-3-73 | Second injury involving loss or loss of use of eye or member, when combined with pre-existing loss or loss or use, causes permanent total disability | Resultant disability from second injury. | Difference between payment for second injury and permanent total disability. | Up to $200,000 may be transferred from the Administrative Expenses Fund. $300 in dependency death cases. $500 in no-dependence death cases. | When fund reaches $300,000 payments are suspended, and reinstated when fund reaches $150,000 |
| Missouri Stat. ref: 287.220, 287.715 | Previous partial permanent industrial disability of at least 12 ½% body as a whole or 15% of major extremity exists, and presents additional disability of at least 12 ½% body as a whole or 15% of major extremity exists. | Resultant disability from second injury | Difference between payment for second injury and combined disability | Surcharge set annually as a percentage of premiums paid by all insured and self insured premium equivalent. | |
| Montana Stat. ref: 39-71-907 | Second injury, when added to certified pre-existing physical impairment, which results in disability or death. | Medical benefits for 104 weeks following the injury and the first 104 weeks of indemnity benefits. | Reimbursement of employer after first 104 weeks. | Surcharge of employers. | Worker must be certified as vocationally handicapped. |
| Nebraska | | Successive Injury Fund Eliminated | | | |
| Nevada | Nevada administers four separate successive injury funds, each with different qualifications and requirements. | | | | |
| New Hampshire Stat. ref: 281-A:54 | Second injury, when added to pre-existing physical impairment, which results in greater disability. | Disability benefits for the first 104 weeks. | Reimbursement for employers after the first 104 weeks, plus 50% of anything over $10,000 during the first 104 weeks. | Assessment against insurers and self-insurers. | An employer is reimbursed 50% of cost of modification if it makes modification to retain an injured worker, not to exceed $5,000 yearly per employee. |
| New Jersey Stat. ref: 34:15-94 and 95 | Second injury, when added to pre-existing partial disability, which results in total disability. | Resultant disability from second injury. | Difference between payment for second injury and pre-existing disability. | Annual surcharge on policyholders and assessment of self-insurers. | Up to $12,500 per year may be transferred to the fund for administrative expenses. |
| New Mexico | | Successive Injury Fund Eliminated | | | |
| New York Workers Comp code: 15 | Second injury, when pre-existing permanent physical impairment results in a permanent disability caused by materially and substantially greater conditions than that which have resulted from the second injury alone. | Benefits for death or disability for first 260 weeks | Reimbursement of employer after first 260 weeks | Assessment against carriers and self-insurers. | |

| State | Covered Injuries | Employer Obligation | Fund Obligation | Fund Sources | Other Provisions |
|---|---|---|---|---|---|
| North Carolina Stat. ref: 97-35 | Second injury involving loss of eye or member, when combined with pre-existing injury results in permanent total disability, provided the prior and subsequent disability were each 20% of the entire member. | Resultant disability from second injury. | Difference between payment for second injury and permanent total disability. | Employer of insurer assessments. | |
| North Dakota | | Monopolistic State Fund | | | |
| Ohio Stat. ref: 4123.343 | Second injury aggravates pre-existing condition or disease and causes death, temporary or permanent total disability, and disability compensable under a particular schedule. | Resultant disability from occupational disease or injury sustained in employment | Determined by Bureau. | Statutory surplus funds | |
| Oklahoma Stat. ref: title 85§172-3 | Second injury to physically impaired person that causes additional permanent disability, and where the combination results in greater disability than would have resulted from second injury alone. | Disability from latest injury to the extent that of injury as if there had been no prior impairment. | Liability for combined disabilities, either permanent total or permanent partial. | Diversion of funds, temporary assessments and taxes. | Fund is now called Multiple Injury Trust Fund. |
| Oregon Stat. ref: 656.628 | Any new compensable injury. | First $1000 of expenses. | Payment determined by Bureau; subsequent injuries throughout the claimant's working career as the result of the condition. | Percentage of hourly wages paid by the worker and employer | Reimbursement from fund requires approval from department. |
| Pennsylvania Stat. ref: title 77, § 516 and 517 | Second injury involving loss or loss of use, when added to a pre-existing loss or loss of use of a hand, arm, foot, leg or eye, causes total disability. | Resultant disability as a result of second injury according to schedule of benefits. | Any remaining compensation due to total disability. | Assessment against carriers and self-insurers. | |
| Rhode Island | | Successive Injury Fund Eliminated | | | |
| South Carolina Stat. ref: 42-9-400, 42-7-310 | Second injury, when combined with any prior permanent physical impairment, results in substantially greater disability or death. | The first 78 weeks of disability compensation and medical care caused by second injury | Reimbursement of employer for all benefits after 78 weeks, plus 50% of medical payments over $3,000 during the first 78 weeks. | Assessment of carriers and self-insurers. | Employer must prove prior knowledge of impairment or that worker was unaware of impairment. |
| South Dakota | | Successive Injury Fund Eliminated | | | |

| State | Covered Injuries | Employer Obligation | Fund Obligation | Fund Sources | Other Provisions |
|-------|------------------|---------------------|-----------------|--------------|------------------|
| Tennessee Stat. ref: 50-6-208 | Second injury, when added to pre-existing impairment or disability, results in permanent total disability. | Resultant disability from second injury. | Benefits exceeding 100% total disability to body as a whole. | Premium tax on insurers and self-insurers. | Employer must prove knowledge of pre-existing disability. |
| Texas Stat. ref: 403.006, 403.007 | Subsequent compensable injury added to the effects of a previous injury. | Benefits that would have accrued if only the subsequent injury had occurred and not the previous injury. | Balance of lifetime income benefits. | Maintenance tax, and 364 weeks no dependency death case benefits. | |
| Utah | | | Successive Injury Fund Eliminated | | |
| Vermont | | | Successive Injury Fund Eliminated | | |
| Virginia Stat. ref: 65.2-1100-1105 | Second injury involving 20% loss or loss of use of eye or member, when combined with pre-existing disability of 20% or more, and causes partial or total disability. | Resultant disability from second injury. | Pro-rata reimbursement to employer for compensation has expired, and up to $7,500 for vocational and medical rehabilitation expenses. | Premium tax on carriers and self-insurers. | Payments are suspended when the fund reaches $250,000 and reinstated when the funds drop to $125,000. |
| Washington Stat. ref: 51.16.120 | Second injury or disease, which, when added to pre-existing injury or disease, causes permanent total disability or death. | Resultant disability from second injury | Difference between charge assessed against employer at time of second injury and total cost of pension reserve. | Transfer from accident fund and self-insurers assessments. | |
| West Virginia Stat. ref: 23-3-1 | Second injury, when combined with prior disabilities, results in permanent total disability. | Resultant disability from second injury. | Remainder of compensation due for permanent total disability. | Assessment of self-insurers. | Self-insurers required to subscribe to Second Injury Fund. |
| Wisconsin Stat ref: 102.59 | Second injury with permanent disability for 200 weeks or more, with a pre-existing disability of 200 weeks or more. | Resultant disability from second injury. | The disability caused by the lesser of two injuries. If the combined disabilities cause permanent total disability, the fund pays the difference between compensation for second injury and permanent total disability. | $10,000 for loss of hand, arm, foot, leg, or eye. | |
| Wyoming | | | No Successive Injury Fund | | |

# TYPE OF LAW BY STATE

| Jurisdiction | Type of Law | Waivers Permitted | State Fund | Pvt. Carrier |
|---|---|---|---|---|
| Alabama | Compulsory | No | No | Yes |
| Alaska | Compulsory | Yes | No | Yes |
| Arizona | Compulsory | Yes | Competitive | Yes |
| Arkansas | Compulsory | Yes | No | Yes |
| California | Compulsory | No | Competitive | Yes |
| Colorado | Compulsory | Yes | Competitive | Yes |
| Connecticut | Compulsory | Yes | No | Yes |
| Delaware | Compulsory | No | No | Yes |
| Dist. of Col. | Compulsory | No | No | Yes |
| Florida | Compulsory | Yes | No | Yes |
| Georgia | Compulsory | Yes | No | Yes |
| Hawaii | Compulsory | No | Competitive | Yes |
| Idaho | Compulsory | No | Competitive | Yes |
| Illinois | Compulsory | No | No | Yes |
| Indiana | Compulsory | No | No | Yes |
| Iowa | Compulsory | Yes | No | Yes |
| Kansas | Compulsory | Yes | No | Yes |
| Kentucky | Compulsory | Yes | Competitive | Yes |
| Louisiana | Compulsory | Yes | Competitive | Yes |
| Maine | Compulsory | Yes | Competitive | Yes |
| Maryland | Compulsory | Yes | Competitive | Yes |
| Massachusetts | Compulsory | No | No | Yes |
| Michigan | Compulsory | Yes | Competitive | Yes |
| Minnesota | Compulsory | No | Competitive | Yes |
| Mississippi | Compulsory | No | No | Yes |
| Missouri | Compulsory | No | Competitive | Yes |
| Montana | Compulsory | Yes | Competitive | Yes |
| Nebraska | Compulsory | Yes | No | Yes |
| Nevada | Compulsory | No | No | Yes |
| New Hampshire | Compulsory | No | No | Yes |
| New Jersey[1,2] | Compulsory | No | No | Yes |
| New Mexico | Compulsory | Yes | Competitive | Yes |
| New York | Compulsory | No | Competitive | Yes |
| North Carolina | Compulsory | Yes | No | Yes |
| North Dakota | Compulsory | No | Exclusive | No |
| Ohio | Compulsory | Yes | Exclusive | No |
| Oklahoma | Compulsory | No | Competitive | Yes |

| Jurisdiction | Type of Law | Waivers Permitted | State Fund | Pvt. Carrier |
|---|---|---|---|---|
| Oregon | Compulsory | No | Competitive | Yes |
| Pennsylvania | Compulsory | No | Competitive | Yes |
| Puerto Rico | Compulsory | No | Exclusive | No |
| Rhode Island | Compulsory | No | Competitive | Yes |
| South Carolina | Compulsory | Yes | No | Yes |
| South Dakota | Compulsory | Yes | No | Yes |
| Tennessee | Compulsory | Yes | No | Yes |
| Texas[3] | Elective | No | Competitive | Yes |
| Utah | Compulsory | No | Competitive | Yes |
| Vermont | Compulsory | Yes | No | Yes |
| Virginia | Compulsory | Yes | No | Yes |
| Virgin Islands | Compulsory | No | Exclusive | No |
| Washington | Compulsory | No | Exclusive | No |
| West Virginia | Compulsory | No | Exclusive | Yes |
| Wisconsin | Compulsory | No | No | Yes |
| Wyoming[4] | Compulsory | No | Exclusive | No |
| | | | | |
| United States *: | | | | |
|   FECA | Compulsory | No | Exclusive | No |
|   LHWCA | Compulsory | No | No | Yes |

\* Federal Employee's Compensation Act.
  Longshore and Harbor Workers' Compensation Act.

## **FOOTNOTES**

[1]New Jersey: Workers compensation coverage may be terminated by either party upon sixty days notice in writing prior to any accident.

[2]New Jersey: Permits ten or more employers licensed by the State as hospitals to group self-insure.

[3]Texas: Provides for mandatory workers' compensation coverage under Title 25 of State statutes regarding rules and regulations for "Carriers" (Article 911-A, Sec. II, Motor Bus Transportation and Regulations by the Railroad Commission).

[4]Wyoming: The law is compulsory for all employers engaged in extra-hazardous occupations and elective for all other occupations.

# Index